REVEALED! The precise location of the garage where Apple was started and the identity of the forgotten founder who walked away from hundreds of millions of dollars. **See page 1**

HATE TO BREAK IT TO YOU, but the Mac wasn't Steve Jobs' idea at all. In fact, he tried killing the project in its infancy. Meet the real father of the Mac, with a first-hand account of where the name Macintosh came from. **See page 84**

DISCOVER the outrageously short-sighted decisions—such as Commodore passing up the opportunity to buy Apple, and Apple declining to purchase VisiCalc—guaranteed to leave you slapping your forehead and asking, "What *were* they thinking?!" **See page 10**

Find out why savvy businessman Bill Gates now considers forcing Apple to kill MacBASIC "one of the stupidest deals I have ever done."

SALIVATE OVER the incredible fortunes made by the fortunate founders, and find out how Wozniak took care of the many people Jobs neglected. **See page 37**

"Trying to have a conversation with Steve Jobs is like trying to take a sip from a fire hose."

Fred Hoar, former VP of communications at Apple
Accidental Millionaire, p. 154-155

WE BLOW THE LID OFF the oft-repeated myth that the famous *1984* commercial only aired once. As an added bonus, the text of Big Brother's speech is included in its entirety. **See page 114**

Peruse detailed timelines of the major events in history of personal computing, including the development of Macintosh, Lisa, Apple III, NeXT, Windows, and more.

BOOKS THAT WORK JUST LIKE YOUR MAC

As a Macintosh user, you enjoy unique advantages. You enjoy a dynamic user environment. You enjoy the successful integration of graphics, sound, and text. Above all, you enjoy a computer that's fun and easy to use.

When your computer gives you all this, why accept less in your computer books?

At SYBEX, we don't believe you should. That's why we've committed ourselves to publishing the highest quality computer books for Macintosh users. Externally, our books emulate the Mac "look and feel," with powerful, appealing illustrations and easy-to-read pages. Internally, our books stress "why" over "how," so you'll learn concepts, not sequences of steps. Philosophically, our books are designed to help you get work done, not to teach you about computers.

In short, our books are fun and easy to use—just like the Mac. We hope you find them just as enjoyable.

For a complete catalog of our publications:

SYBEX Inc.
2021 Challenger Drive, Alameda, CA 94501
Tel: (510) 523-8233/ (800) 227-2346 Telex: 336311
Fax: (510) 523-2373

SYBEX is committed to using natural resources wisely to preserve and improve our environment. As a leader in the computer book publishing industry, we are aware that over 40% of America's solid waste is paper. This is why we have been printing the text of books like this one on recycled paper since 1982.

This year our use of recycled paper will result in the saving of more than 15,300 trees. We will lower air pollution effluents by 54,00 pounds, save 6,300,00 gallons of water, and reduce landfill by 2,700 cubic yards.

In choosing a SYBEX book you are not only making a choice for the best in skills and information, you are also choosing to enhance the quality of life for all of us.

TALK TO SYBEX ONLINE.

JOIN THE SYBEX FORUM ON COMPUSERVE®

- Talk to SYBEX authors, editors and fellow forum members.
- Get tips, hints, and advice online.
- Download shareware and the source code from SYBEX books.

If you're already a CompuServe user, just enter GO SYBEX to join the SYBEX Forum. If you're not, try CompuServe free by calling 1-800-848-8199 and ask for Representative 560. You'll get one free month of basic service and a $15 credit for CompuServe extended services—a $23.95 value. Your personal ID number and password will be activated when you sign up.

Join us online today. Enter GO SYBEX on CompuServe. If you're not a CompuServe member, call Representative 560 at 1-800-848-8199

(outside U.S./Canada call 614-457-0802)

SYBEX
Shortcuts to
Understanding

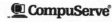

The Mac® Bathroom Reader

Owen W. Linzmayer

SYBEX®

San Francisco ■ *Paris* ■ *Düsseldorf* ■ *Soest*

Acquisitions Editor: Joanne Cuthbertson
Developmental Editor: Steve Lipson
Editor: Alex Miloradovich
Project Editor: Kristen Vanberg-Wolff
Book Designer: Suzanne Albertson
Illustrator: Cuong Le
Cartoonist: Michael Kim
Production Services: Penn&Ink
Page Layout: Sandra Page Taylor, Dayna Goforth
Graphics File Manager: Aldo X. Bermudez
Proofreader/Production Assistants: John Selawsky, Lisa Haden
Indexer: Matthew Spence
Cover Designer: Joanna Kim Gladden
Cover Photographer: Robert Sondgroth
SYBEX is a registered trademark of SYBEX Inc.

Library of Congress Card Number: 94-67199

ISBN: 0-7821-1531-4

Manufactured in the United States of America

10 9 8 7 6 5 4 3 2 1

*Dedicated to my wife, Alane, and to my cat, Nutella,
neither of whom read in the bathroom.
It must be a guy thing...*

Acknowledgments

While the cover of this book bears my name alone, I could not have written it without the contributions of many others to whom I am deeply indebted. (Yeah, I know I always say the exact same thing in every book I write, but it's the truth!) Foremost, I'd like to thank Steve Lipson, my developmental editor at SYBEX, for originally proposing the idea of a Macintosh bathroom reader. Let's hope my implementation lives up to his inspiration.

Special thanks goes to Jane Oros and David Thomas Craig. Jane granted me unrestricted access to the corporate library at Apple Computer and was always willing to help track down an elusive fact. David is an independent Lisa enthusiast who provided me with more pre-Mac information than any human really needs to know, and graciously read through some of my early drafts to prevent embarrassing errors from making it into print.

I'd also like to thank the many individuals who helped by offering information, content, leads, and suggestions for improving the book you now hold in your hands: Peter Baum (Ninth Wave), Christopher Breen, Wayne Cooper (Farrand Cooper & Bruiniers), Greg Cornelison (Claris), Donn Denman (The 3DO Company), Chris Espinosa (Apple Computer), Jonathan Fitch (Apple Computer), Bill Griffis (Standard & Poors Compustat), Galen Gruman (Macworld), Martin P. Haeberli (Apple Computer), Rhona Hamilton (Macworld), Mark Harlan (Apple Computer), Trip Hawkins (The 3DO Company), Steve Hayden (BBDO), Camille Johnson (Goldberg Moser O'Neill), Cathy King (BBDO), Daniel G. Kottke (Pollstar Systems), Marianne Lettieri (Apple Computer), Steven Levy

(Macworld), Alex Louie (Berkeley Systems), Alfred J. Mandel (Big Idea Group), Mike Markkula (Apple Computer), Doug McKenna (Mathemaethetics), Dan Muse (Macworld), Richard O'Neil (Chiat/Day), Carol Parcels (Hewlett-Packard), Ben Pang (Apple Computer), Eric Perret (Esquire), Jef Raskin, Heidi Roizen (T/Maker), David Roots (Radius), Ken Rothmuller (Hewlett-Packard), Michael M. Scott (White Rose), Erica Stearns (Standard & Poors Compustat), Jeff Sullivan, Michael Swaine, Marcio Luis Teixeira, and Steve Wozniak. Those are just the names that I remembered to jot down and who agreed to speak on the record. To everyone whose name I forgot or was asked not to publish, thank you too.

And of course, thanks to everyone who has ever worked at Apple. Without you there would be no Macintosh and the world of computing wouldn't be nearly as enjoyable.

Owen W. Linzmayer
San Francisco, California

Contents

Introduction   xxii

Ron Wayne: The Forgotten Founder   1

What Were They Thinking?   10

Broken Breakout Promises   22

Code Names Uncovered   25

The Apple III Fiasco   28

Millionaire Mania   37

Taking Stock of Apple   44

IBM: The Strangest Bedfellow of All   47

Lisa: From Xerox with Love   59

Folon's Forgotten Logo   81

The Making of Macintosh   84

*1984: The Greatest Commercial That
Almost Never Aired*   114

The Mac Meets the Press   127

Bold Intros and Quiet Exits   136

*Billion-Dollar Bill and His Amazing
American Express Card*   142

Lemmings: Why 1985 Wasn't Like 1984   145

Looney Licenses   152

*The Remarkable Rise and Fabulous Fall
of John Sculley*   156

Stupid Mac Stories   173

The Great Caffeine Conspiracy   185

What's in a Name?   188

The Official History of the Dogcow   216

Easter Egg Hunt   227

Taking Trademarks to the Bank   238

Windows: How Sculley Betrayed the Mac   244

Jobs after Apple: NeXT to NoTHING   255

Macintosh Insiders: Where Are They Now?   272

Bibliography   290

Index   293

Introduction

Welcome to *The Mac Bathroom Reader*, an irreverent history of Apple Computer, focusing on the events, people, products, and companies that made the Macintosh what it is today. As you can surmise from the title, this isn't yet another how-to or tips & tricks book that requires you to be seated at your computer while you read it. Nah, there are enough of those on the market already. This book is a unique collection of amazing anecdotes, interesting lists, exploded myths, silly stories, embarrassing quotes, and other useless factoids meant to be enjoyed at your leisure, wherever you happen to enjoy reading. The random-access layout and short-attention-span story sizes, however, make this tome particularly well suited to reading in that all-American sanctum of intellectual pursuit, the bathroom. Whether perused in bits and pieces during periodic trips to the throne, or consumed in a single marathon session following an unfortunate bout of Montezuma's Revenge, I hope you find *The Mac Bathroom Reader* both fascinating, factual, and fair. Enjoy!

Owen W. Linzmayer

2227 15th Avenue

San Francisco, CA 94116-1824

AppleLink: Owen

America Online: Owen Ink

CompuServe: 71333,3152

Ron Wayne: The Forgotten Founder

Thanks to a never-ending campaign by Apple's powerful public relations machine to protect the myths surrounding the company's origin, almost everyone believes that Apple was started in a garage by "the two Steves," Stephen Gary Wozniak and Steven Paul Jobs. Actually, the operation began in a bedroom at 11161 Crist Drive in Los Altos (the house number changed to 2066 when the land was annexed from the county to the city in late

Courtesy of Michael Swaine

Steve Jobs in "the garage" on Crist Drive in Los Altos, California (inset: the house as it is today).

1

1983), where Jobs—after having dropped out of Reed College—was living with his adoptive parents, Paul R. and Clara Jobs. But that mere semantic distinction can be forgiven. When the bedroom became too crowded, the operation indeed moved to the garage.

The bigger story here is that the two Steves weren't alone in forming Apple. Just as Soviet propagandists doctored photos to remove party members who had fallen out of

Ron Wayne, the forgotten founder.

favor, Apple suffers from a convenient case of institutional amnesia by routinely ignoring the fact that when Apple was originally founded as a partnership on April Fools' Day, 1976, there were three founders: Woz, Jobs, and a fellow by the name of Ron Wayne. An eccentric arch-conservative, Wayne was a chief field service engineer who had worked with Steve Jobs at Atari, but Jobs convinced him to join Apple by offering him 10 percent of the stock.

While Wayne was working at his home on the original Apple logo and documentation for the Apple I, Jobs was hustling up customers. At a Homebrew Computer Club meeting in May 1976, Jobs gave a demonstration of the Apple I to Paul Terrell, who operated the Byte Shop, the first retail computer store chain in the country. Terrell was intrigued and asked Jobs to keep in touch.

The next day, Jobs dropped in on Terrell at his store in Mountain View, California and exclaimed, "I'm keeping in touch." To Jobs' utter amazement, Terrell promised to buy 50 computers for $500 each, cash on delivery. There was only one catch: Terrell wanted fully-assembled computers.

Courtesy of Apple Computer, Inc.

The Byte Shop was Apple's first big customer.

"That was the biggest single epi-
sode in the company's history,"
says Woz. "Nothing in subsequent years was so great and so
unexpected. It was not what we
had intended to do."

The Little Kingdom, p. 142

The trio had originally planned to produce bare circuit boards for $25 each and sell them for $50 to hobbyists who would populate them with the necessary chips and other parts. They didn't have the money necessary to buy all of the parts required to build 50 complete computers, but Jobs was undaunted. Through sheer force of will, he managed to convince suppliers to give him parts on 30 days' credit.

The troika got help from Bill Fernandez, who had origi-nally introduced Jobs to Woz in 1968, as well as Daniel G. Kottke, who had met Jobs at Reed College and trav-eled to India with him. Everyone worked furiously to build the computers by hand. Terrell was a bit dismayed when Jobs showed up on the 29th day to deliver a batch of motherboards stuffed with components. When Terrell asked for "fully-assembled" computers, he meant the whole works: a case, power supply, monitor, and key-board. Nonetheless, Terrell kept his word and paid cash. Apple was able to pay off the parts suppliers just in time.

Jobs was excited. Apple had turned a decent profit and he had plans to expand the business by going into debt

Courtesy of Apple Computer, Inc.

The original Apple I (shown here in a custom-built wooden case) was little more than a circuit board to which customers were expected to add a case, power supply, monitor and keyboard.

with parts suppliers to build even more computers. Wayne would have none of that. Jobs had a vision of a huge market for personal computers, but all Wayne could focus on was the fact that he would be responsible for 10 percent of any debts Apple incurred. He had already been burned investing in several other Silicon Valley start-ups, so shortly after filling the initial Byte Shop order, Wayne wrote a formal letter of resignation and renounced his interest in the company, hoping that would absolve him of all responsibility.

"I had already learned what gave me indigestion and I was beginning to feel the months running by. If Apple had failed, I would have had bruises on top of bruises. Steve Jobs was an absolute whirlwind and I had lost the energy you need to ride whirlwinds." (*The Little Kingdom*, p. 150)

According to *So Far*, an Apple-sponsored vanity coffee-table book published upon the 10-year anniversary of the company's founding, Wayne received $500 for his share of the company, which he used to open a coin shop.

> ### Why did you send me this renegade from the human race?
>
> **Don Valentine,** venture capitalist, complaining about Steve Jobs, then a smelly kid with ripped jeans and bare feet.
>
> (*West of Eden,* p. 34)

Jobs' ambitious plans required more money than the Apple I orders were generating, so in August 1976, he approached his old Atari boss, Nolan K. Bushnell, who recommended he meet with venture capitalist Don Valentine. At the time Valentine wasn't interested, but he in turn referred Jobs to Armas Clifford "Mike" Markkula Jr., who had retired after making his fortune at Intel and Fairchild Semiconductor.

Markkula came out of retirement to help Jobs devise a business plan. He was so impressed with the potential of Jobs and Woz, he invested $92,000 in cash and committed up to $250,000 if necessary. Now, properly funded, the three of them incorporated Apple Computer on January 3, 1977. To avoid any possible legal complications, in March the corporation purchased the partnership for $5,308.96 and Wayne was sent a check for a third of that amount to make certain he would have no future claim against the company. Wayne, who had walked away voluntarily, was thrilled to receive this

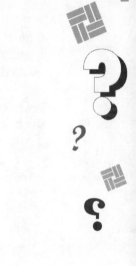

Courtesy of Apple Computer, Inc.

Armas Clifford "Mike" Markkula Jr.
stepped in when Ron Wayne stepped out.

Reflecting on the situation, Woz understands Wayne's decision to bail out early. "Steve had no money. I had no money, and the creditors were going to wind up coming to him for the money that was going to be owed. So he decided it was better to get out of it. At the time it was the right decision." To someone who was there to witness the events firsthand, it may have made sense, but in retrospect, it's hard for an outsider to see Wayne's decision as anything but a mistake of colossal proportions.

At the close of the 1993 fiscal year, 10 percent of all outstanding shares in Apple had a market value of over $290 million. Even though Apple stock was trading at a historically low price at that time, it's certainly a sizable enough chunk of change to make you wonder if Ron Wayne ever regrets relinquishing his supporting role in one of the greatest American business success stories ever told.

The Apple Logo

One of Ron Wayne's first duties when he joined Apple was to design a logo for the infant company. The logo he created was a pen-and-ink drawing of Newton leaning against an apple tree with a portion of a William Wordsworth poem (the Prelude, Book III, Residence of Cambridge) running around the border.

Apple's original logo was designed by Ron Wayne.

Wayne's logo was used for a short time, but Jobs eventually came to feel that it was too cerebral and not easily reproduced at small sizes, so he instructed Rob Janov, an art director at the Regis McKenna public relations agency, to come up with a better logo. Janov started with a black & white silhouette of an apple, but something was still missing. "I wanted to simplify the shape of an apple, and by taking a bite—a byte, right?—out of the side, it prevented the apple from looking like a cherry tomato," explains Janov.

8

Courtesy of Apple Computer, Inc.

For a touch of class, Janov added six colorful, horizontal stripes. Although separating the colors with thin black lines would have reduced registration problems during reproduction, Jobs nixed the proposal, resulting in the Apple logo as we know it today, which former president Michael M. Scott calls "the most expensive bloody logo ever designed."

"One of the deep mysteries to me is our logo, the symbol of lust and knowledge, bitten into, all crossed with the colors of the rainbow in the wrong order. You couldn't dream of a more appropriate logo: lust, knowledge, hope, and anarchy."

Jean-Louis Gassée,
former president
of Apple Products
Odyssey, p. 280 and *So Far*, p. 141

9

What Were They Thinking?

Looking back over the years, it's interesting (and perhaps even a bit gratifying) to see that supposedly sagacious professionals and sophisticated institutions made outrageously short-sighted decisions at momentous occasions during the development of the microcomputer industry. Recounted here for your reading pleasure are just a few tales of woe guaranteed to leave you slapping your forehead and asking, "What *were* they thinking?!"

"It's not like we were all smart enough to see a revolution coming. Back then, I thought there might be a revolution in opening your garage door, balancing your checkbook, keeping your recipes, that sort of thing. There are a million people who study markets and analyze economic trends, people who are more brilliant than I am, people who worked for companies like Digital Equipment and IBM and Hewlett-Packard. None of them foresaw what was going to happen, either."

Steve Wozniak
So Far, p. 140

Hewlett-Packard

Courtesy of Hewlett-Packard Co.

After creating the prototype of the original Apple I computer in his spare time during March 1976, Steve Wozniak approached his employer, Hewlett-Packard, and tried to convince it to consider making microcomputers. "I pitched my boss, the calculator lab manager, and got him all excited, but it was obvious it didn't have a place at HP," recalls Woz.

Although his boss didn't think the Apple I was appropriate for his division, he instructed an HP lawyer to call each division head asking, "You interested in an $800 machine that can run BASIC and hook up to a TV?" Everyone declined, saying "HP doesn't want to be in that kind of market."

Eventually HP would change its mind and produce its own line of personal computers, but with a release letter from HP in hand, Woz was free to go off and market the Apple I on his own time. What makes the story all the more ironic is that HP itself had been started by William Hewlett and David Packard in a garage at 367 Addison Avenue in Palo Alto (now a state historical landmark), not far from Steve Jobs' boyhood home.

Atari

ATARI®

Courtesy of Atari Corporation

Steve Wozniak was pretty comfortable pulling down $24,000 annually with his job at Hewlett-Packard, and he wasn't about to quit to sell the bare Apple I circuit board to hobbyists. He didn't share Steve Jobs' vision of a huge personal computer marketplace, nor did he have the ambition to build his own company to exploit it. So after discussing the matter with Jobs, they approached Atari, where Jobs worked as a technician.

"After we had the Apple I built on a board, we showed it to Al Alcorn of Atari," recalls Woz. "Atari had just come out with their first Home Pong game and it was going to be so big that they had their hands full. They thought the Apple I was a great thing, but they had plenty going themselves."

So, like Hewlett-Packard before it, Atari decided not to buy out Apple. Of course, Atari went on to dominate the early home video game market, selling 150,000 Home Pongs in its first year (incidentally, Home Pong was code-named Darleen, after an Atari employee).

Atari was itself purchased by Warner Communications for $28 million in 1976, and eventually entered the home computer market with its own line of computers.

Courtesy of Atari Corporation

Although it passed on the Apple I, Atari eventually sold its own line of computers (shown here, the Atari 800).

Commodore Business Machines

Courtesy of Commodore Business Machines Inc.

Spurned by both of their employers, Woz and Jobs decided to go it alone. To scrape together the $1,350 cost of producing the original Apple I printed circuit board, Woz sold his Hewlett-Packard 65 programmable calculator for $250 and Jobs sold his red and white Volkswagen bus for $1,500. By all accounts, the Apple I was only a moderate success, selling about 200 units in all.

"We were real small-time operators, kind of like somebody who sold arts and crafts on the side," admits Woz.

But after building the Apple II prototype, they realized they had a big winner on their hands. Unfortunately, they lacked the funds to turn it into a success. The Apple I was relatively inexpensive to build, and it generated just enough income to sustain itself. In contrast, the Apple II cost several hundred dollars each to produce. "How do you build 1,000 of something that costs a lot of money?" Woz asks rhetorically. "We didn't have any money."

Knowing that Commodore was anxious to get into the nascent microcomputer market, Jobs invited a couple of representatives to come to his parent's garage and see the Apple II breadboard putting high-resolution color spirals on the screen, an impressive feat in the fall of 1976. Commodore was interested and Jobs offered to sell the company for $100,000 in cash, some Commodore stock, and salaries of $36,000 a year for himself and Wozniak.

"I thought it was atrocious. I had put a man-year of work into it, and I thought it was grossly outrageous to ask for so much," recalls Woz. Nonetheless, he would have gladly taken the deal because his passion was building computers, not companies. His father, Jerry, was also appalled by Jobs' demands, but not for the same reasons. He felt that Jobs was taking advantage of his son's work.

"You didn't do shit."

Jerry Wozniak to Steve Jobs,
when he found out that Jobs
expected an even split.
Accidental Millionaire, p. 78

To his credit, one thing Jobs did do was investigate their suitor. "The more I looked into Commodore, the sleazier they were. I couldn't find one person who had made a deal with them and was happy. Everyone felt they had been cheated," said Jobs. (*The Little Kingdom*, p. 161)

Fortunately for Apple, Commodore founder Jack Tramiel thought it was ridiculous to acquire two guys working out of a garage. Instead, in October 1976, Commodore bought MOS Technology, the firm that developed the inexpensive 6502 microprocessor that was the heart of the Apple II.

Chuck Peddle, the engineer who designed the 6502, slapped together the Commodore PET in four months. Peddle admits the frivolous name was inspired by the Pet Rock craze of the era, although the acronym officially stood for Personal Electronic Transactor.

The boxy PET was an all-in-one computer with a built-in display, cassette deck, and keyboard, but it was the stuff it didn't include that caused many industry insiders to deride the kludgy machine as Peddle's Ego Trip. Recalls Woz, "They left out expandability, color, good memory, high-resolution graphics, a nice keyboard, the ability to use your TV...all sorts of things." Considering the relative lifespans of the PET versus the Apple II, it's doubtful Jack Tramiel can ever forget his mistake in passing up Apple.

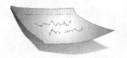

RIP: Commodore announced plans to go out of business April 29, 1994.

15

Instead of buying Apple, Commodore bought MOS Technology which designed the PET.

VisiCalc

HP, Atari, and Commodore aren't the only companies that failed to recognize a good thing when they saw it. Apple is guilty of passing up tremendous opportunities itself. Case in point, VisiCalc.

In January of 1979, Daniel Fylstra, from Boston-based Personal Software, Inc., showed Mike Markkula and Steve Jobs a prototype of an Applesoft BASIC program called Calculedger. Written in an attic by 26-year-old Daniel Bricklin, a Harvard Business School MBA student, and his friend Robert Frankston, Calculedger was a cross between a calculator and a ledger sheet which solved complex "what if" financial-planning problems by establishing mathematical relationships between numbers.

Courtesy of Michael Swaine

Dan Bricklin, author of VisiCalc, one of the best-selling computer programs of all time.

Fylstra offered to sell this revolutionary program for $1 million, but Apple turned him down. The wizards in Cupertino were not alone in failing to grasp the importance of the program. Bill Gates also declined to purchase the program because Microsoft was too busy selling BASIC directly to computer manufacturers to get involved in publishing applications, stating "We do not talk to any end users."

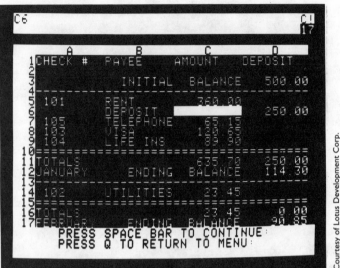

The first version of VisiCalc wasn't much to look at, but the world had never seen anything like it.

By the time it was unveiled publicly at the West Coast Computer Faire in San Francisco that May, Calculedger had been renamed VisiCalc (a contraction of visible calculator) and the world got its first look at an electronic spreadsheet. When finally published in October 1979, VisiCalc ran on the Apple II only and helped launch that machine as the business standard because finally a computer could do something extremely useful.

VisiCalc was arguably the first "killer application" that was so compelling that people bought hardware just to run it. It went on to become one of the hottest-selling software products in the personal computer industry.

Missed Windows of Opportunity

Personal Software was ultimately renamed VisiCorp in recognition of its reliance on its flagship product. VisiCorp would again impress the world at the 1982 Fall Comdex in Las Vegas by demonstrating VisiOn (code-named Quasar), a graphical user interface for souped-up IBM PCs. Keep in mind, Apple hadn't even announced Lisa yet, so this was most people's first look at a WIMP system (windows, icons, mice, and pop-up menus).

Unfortunately for VisiCorp, its window of opportunity had already shut when VisiOn shipped a year later. Since VisiOn couldn't run DOS applications, to make it useful you had to shell out a total of $1,765 for a package which included a spreadsheet, graphing program, word processor, and mouse. In addition to being late and overpriced, VisiOn was slow, buggy, and had onerous hardware requirements. In August 1983, Control Data bought VisiOn and it was never heard of again.

MacBASIC

Some analysts credit Microsoft's current dominance in the industry to the wisdom and ruthless business practices of its founder and chairman, William Henry Gates III. But even big bad Bill has blundered and perhaps never more so than when it came to the curious case of MacBASIC.

In August 1977, Apple agreed to pay $21,000 for an eight-year license to Microsoft's version of BASIC, which after some fiddling by a high-school kid named Randy Wigginton (who went on to create MacWrite), was released as Applesoft BASIC and burned into the ROMs of every Apple II. Mindful of the role BASIC played in the success of the Apple II, in 1982 Steve Jobs encouraged Microsoft to develop a BASIC programming language for the Macintosh. Subsequently he instructed programmer Donn Denman to begin work on Apple's own implementation called MacBASIC, which was originally scheduled to ship in the second quarter of 1984 for $99.

Anxious to reap the financial rewards of being first to market, Gates rushed Microsoft BASIC to completion and released it upon the introduction of the Mac. By most accounts, Microsoft BASIC was a dog that didn't even take advantage of many of the Mac's unique features such as the powerful Toolbox routines. According to Denman, it was "a really crappy, slow implementation," so he felt confident that he had time to perfect MacBASIC which was widely available in a beta version and receiving very favorable responses.

Gates must have realized that MacBASIC would eat his lunch in the open market, but he had an ace in the hole. When the Applesoft license came up for renewal in 1985, the Apple II line was still the company's cash cow and BASIC was absolutely crucial to the venerable Apple II. Failing to grasp the fact that he had the boys from Cupertino over a barrel and was in the position to extract damn near anything he wanted at the negotiating table, Gates simply demanded that Apple halt development of MacBASIC.

After a fair amount of huffing and puffing, Apple caved in, reasoning that the Mac was designed as an information appliance for which a hobbyist programming language was hardly a necessity. So Apple got off easy by agreeing

Microsoft chairman Bill Gates dictated that Apple kill MacBASIC.

to kill MacBASIC. In exchange, it got a new lease on life for the Apple II and the company.

Microsoft BASIC never set the world on fire (in fact, it was eventually withdrawn in disgrace), but the Apple II continued to contribute significantly to Apple's bottom line for years to come, finally being discontinued officially on November 15, 1993. Gates would later realize the error of his ways and recall that it was "one of the stupidest deals I have ever done."

Incidentally, Denman didn't learn of the deal until Arthur Luehrmann, an outside writer working on a MacBASIC tutorial book, called to tell him that the book the two were collaborating on had been canceled because MacBASIC was deep-sixed.

Broken Breakout Promises

Before there was Apple, Steve Jobs was one of the first 50 employees at Atari, the Silicon Valley game company founded by Nolan K. Bushnell in 1972. Atari's Pong, a simple electronic version of ping-pong, had caught on like wildfire in arcades and homes across the country and Bushnell was anxious to come up with a successor. He envisioned a variation on Pong called Breakout, in which the player bounced a ball off a paddle at the bottom of the screen in an attempt to smash the bricks in a wall at the top.

He turned to Jobs, a technician, to design the circuitry. Initially, Jobs tried to do the work himself, but soon realized he was in over his head and asked his good friend Steve Wozniak to bail him out.

"Steve wasn't capable of designing anything that complex. He came to me and said Atari would like a game and described how it would work," recalls Wozniak. "There was a catch: I had to do it in four days. In retrospect, I think it was because Steve needed the money to buy into a farm up north."

Designing a complex game in such a short period of time was a challenge, so even though Wozniak was working full-time at Hewlett-Packard, he and Jobs put in four all-nighters in a row and finished a working prototype. Both came down with mononucleosis as a result, yet Wozniak remembers it as an incredible experience.

After delivering the game to Atari, Jobs stalled Wozniak, explaining that there was some problem getting the money, but he finally wrote a check for $350 and immediately took off for the All-One Farm in Oregon. Jobs was happy because his friend had helped him get in good with Bushnell. Bushnell was happy because Breakout was designed in record time and used so few chips. And Woz was happy earning some pocket money doing what he loved best. "I would have done it for a quarter," says Wozniak. It wasn't until 1984 that he discovered the truth about the Breakout project and his "good friend," Steve Jobs.

"I was so proud of designing a product like that. Nolan Bushnell wanted a game with as few chips as possible. Steve said if there were less than 50 chips, we got paid $700 and split it in half. Less than 40 chips, $1,000. After four nights, it was 42 chips. I wasn't about to spend another second trying to reduce it by two more chips; I'll settle for $700."

Steve Wozniak

23

"I was on a plane going to a user group club in Fort Lauderdale to promote the Mac, along with some other members of the Mac team," recalls Wozniak. "Andy Hertzfeld had just read *Zap!*, a book about Atari which said that Steve Jobs designed Breakout. I explained to him that we both worked on it and got paid $700. Andy corrected me, 'No, it says here it was $5,000.' When I read in the book how Nolan Bushnell had actually paid Steve $5,000, I just cried."

Certainly it wasn't the money that bothered Woz. Had Jobs asked, Wozniak would have done the project for free because he was turned on by such technological challenges. What really hurt was being betrayed by his friend.

Looking back on the incident, Wozniak realized Jobs' behavior was completely in character. "Steve had worked in surplus electronics and said if you can buy a part for 30¢ and sell it to this guy at the surplus store for $6, you don't have to tell him what you paid for it. It's worth $6 to the guy. And that was his philosophy of running a business," says Wozniak.

Ironically, Woz's design for Breakout was so brilliant that none of the Atari engineers, including Jobs, could figure out exactly how it worked, which made it impossible to test, so the whole thing had to be redesigned in-house before it shipped.

Code Names Uncovered

Apple's new research & development facilities located on Infinite Loop in Cupertino are some of the most secure buildings on the Apple campus. Confidential papers are discarded into locked wastebaskets lest they fall into the hands of dumpster-diving competitors or *MacWEEK* reporters; guards are posted at all entrances; and employees must pass their electronic identification badges in front of wall plates that verify access privileges and monitor personnel movement.

Apple has come a long way from the days when Jobs and Woz eagerly showed off what they were doing in the garage, but it hasn't gotten paranoid. Like all good high-tech companies, Apple is simply trying to maintain the secrecy of the many new technologies and products it is constantly designing.

Before Apple publicly announces a product by its official name, internally it is referred to by a code name. Usually lead engineers or managers get to name their own projects whatever they want, but a few recurring trends are evident. Early in its incarnation, Apple favored female names for projects. More often than not, the projects were named after the children, girlfriends, or wives of the team members (for example, the Lisa was named after Steve Jobs' daughter born out of wedlock).

Jef Raskin rebelled against the sexist notion of female code names and looked instead to apple varieties as the inspiration for his Macintosh project, purposely misspelling McIntosh. For a while, the names of different types of apples (Pippin, Johnathan) were often whispered in the R&D labs.

Having exhausted the apple varieties, project managers now tend to choose whimsical code names that either reflect pop culture or contain awful puns. Perusing the list of code names is like walking down memory lane, checking out the fads and trends that swept through Apple cubicles and lab benches over the years.

Microsoft's Excellent Name

Microsoft Excel was developed under the code name Odyssey (no relation to John Sculley's book, I'm sure), and when it came time to sell the spreadsheet, Microsoft considered calling it Number Buddy, Mr. Spreadsheet, Sigma, and Plansheet, but ultimately it was a district manager who suggested Excel.

Immediately upon Excel's release, Microsoft was sued by Manufacturers Hanover Trust because it owned the rights to the Excel name for its computerized banking service. The two firms eventually settled out of court, with Manufacturers Hanover Trust allowing the use of the word Excel as long as it is always preceded by the name Microsoft.

Gates, pp. 276-277

Apple takes the code-naming business seriously, often assigning the same project different code names, one to be used internally, and another for external use. Also, a single project may have separate code names associated with hardware, software, documentation, and marketing. Furthermore, outsiders—such as developers and the press—may be told about the same project, but each will be told a different code name.

And just to keep everybody guessing, Apple sometimes changes code names in the middle of a project, or reuses old code names for new projects. Not only does all this create confusion in Apple-watchers, it also serves as an audit trail to trace leaks to their sources.

Despite Apple's best efforts to keep a lid on this sort of thing becoming public, after much tedious research I've compiled an exhaustive list of code names that have escaped from Cupertino and other Mac-related firms over the years. In some cases, I've even been able to uncover why a particular code name was chosen. If you've been looking up occasionally while reading this book, you've noticed this list running across the top of every page.

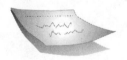

I realize this list isn't perfect, so if you're an Apple employee or devout Mac fan and you spot a code-name error or omission, please bring it to my attention for correction in a subsequent printing.

The Apple III Fiasco

Following two years of development, the Apple III (code-named Sara after chief engineer Wendell Sander's daughter) was announced on May 19, 1980 during the National Computer Conference in Anaheim, California. With Apple's typical flair for spectacle, the company rented out Disneyland for five hours the following night at a cost of $42,000 and transported an estimated 7,000 NCC attendees to the site in British double-decker buses.

Apple was proud of the Apple III because it represented many firsts for the company. Foremost, it was

Courtesy of Apple Computer, Inc.

The Apple III was the firm's first failure.

the company's first attempt at building a powerful business computer. And it was the company's first major departure from the tried-and-true Apple II architecture. It would also prove the company's first bona fide failure. Unfortunately, instead of learning from the experience, Apple repeated many of the same mistakes with the Lisa and the Mac.

The Apple III was sold in two different configurations ranging in price from $4,340 to $7,800. At the heart of each was a Synertek 8-bit 6502A microprocessor running at 2 megahertz (twice the speed of the Apple II), a maximum of 128 kilobytes (K) of random access memory, built-in keyboard with numeric keypad, one internal 143K, 5.25-inch disk drive manufactured by Shugart, and you could add additional devices via the two serial ports. In effect, the Apple III came standard with everything most people eventually added to the Apple II, and if that wasn't enough, there were four internal slots that accepted Apple II peripheral cards.

Although it had an Apple II emulation mode, the Apple III worked best with software written specifically to take advantage of its proprietary Sophisticated Operating System and new features such as a built-in real-time clock and video capable of generating 24 lines of 80-column text and up to 560 by 192 pixels in the monochrome graphics mode. On paper, all the specifications were quite impressive, but implementing them proved a humbling experience for Apple.

> **"We had to put chips in to disable some Apple II features so people's heads would have the right image that Apple IIIs are for business and Apple IIs are for home and hobby."**
>
> **Steve Wozniak**

Apple originally promised to ship the Apple III in July, but production problems plagued the product throughout the summer and into the fall. Unlike the Apple I and II which were essentially the work of one man, Steve Wozniak, the Apple III was designed by a committee headed by Steve Jobs, who would demand one thing today, then the opposite tomorrow. The shipping delays threatened to mar Apple's public offering in December, so managers ignored the dire warnings of engineers who knew what would happen if they pushed the Apple III out the door before its time.

> **"The Apple III was kind of like a baby conceived during a group orgy, and [later] everybody had this bad headache and there's this bastard child, and everyone says, 'It's not mine.'"**
>
> **Randy Wigginton**, who at age sixteen was one of Apple's earliest employees
>
> *Insanely Great*, pp. 123-124

As soon as units began trickling into distribution in late November, the worst fears of the engineers were realized.

On February 10, 1981, Apple announced that the Apple III would no longer contain the much heralded built-in clock/calendar features because National Semiconductor's clock chip didn't meet Apple's specifications. How the flaky parts got into a shipping product nobody was willing to say. Apple dropped the base price of the Apple III to $4,190 and gave a $50 rebate to everybody who had purchased an Apple III up to that date.

When the first volume shipments began in March 1981, it became apparent that dropping the clock chip was just a finger in the dike. Approximately 20 percent of all Apple IIIs were dead on arrival primarily because chips fell out of loose sockets during shipping. Those that did work initially often failed after minimal use thanks to Jobs' insistence that the Apple III not have a fan (a design demand he would make again on the Mac). He reasoned that in addition to reducing radio-frequency interference emissions, the internal aluminum chassis would conduct heat and keep the delicate components cool. He was wrong.

"[Jobs] could see that horizon out there, a thousand miles out. But he could never see the details of each little mile that had to be covered to get there. That was his genius and his downfall."

Jay Elliott, head of human resources at Apple
The Journey Is the Reward,
p. 372

Compounding the problem was that Jobs dictated the size and shape of the case without concern for the demands of the electrical engineers who were then forced to cram boards into small spaces with little or no ventilation and circulation. As the computer was used, the chips got hot, expanded slightly, and slowly worked their way out of their sockets, at which point the computer simply died. As a solution, Apple actually recommended lifting the

Apple III Timeline

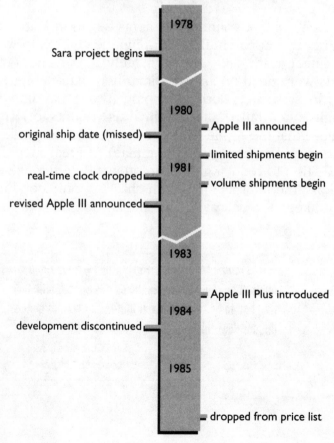

	1978
Sara project begins	
	1980
	Apple III announced
original ship date (missed)	
	limited shipments begin
real-time clock dropped	1981
	volume shipments begin
revised Apple III announced	
	1983
	Apple III Plus introduced
	1984
development discontinued	
	1985
	dropped from price list

32

front of the computer six inches off the desktop, then letting go with the hopes that the chips would reseat themselves.

The problems with loose chips were exacerbated by short cables between internal components and non-gold connectors that suffered from corrosion. To its credit, Apple didn't bury the problem; Mike Markkula, president and CEO, publicly admitted "It would be dishonest for me to sit here and say it's perfect" (*The Wall Street Journal*, April 15, 1981, p. 29). Apple instituted a liberal repair policy, swapping brand new Apple IIIs for bad ones on the spot, no questions asked. Unfortunately, the replacements often failed too.

> **"We had to replace fourteen thousand of them. I must say that, as far as enhancing our reputation, this operation was a success. We received thank-you letters telling us that General Motors would never have done the same."**
>
> **Jean-Louis Gassée**, then general manager of Apple France
> *The Third Apple*, p. 102

On November 9, Apple announced a revised Apple III with a base price of $3,495. The company steadfastly claimed that the original problems were linked to shortcomings in manufacturing and quality-control procedures rather than the underlying design of the computer. Nonetheless, the new Apple III featured different sockets, updated software, memory expansion up to 256K, and an optional 5-megabyte hard disk drive. Based upon the Seagate ST506 mechanism, the $3,495 ProFile was an important addition to the system since IBM didn't yet offer a hard drive for its PC introduced that August (compare $700/MB in 1981 to less than a $1/MB in 1994!). Of the 7,200 original Apple IIIs that had been sold to date, 2,000 were replaced with the new version at no charge when it became available in mid-December.

> **"It just wasn't a good enough machine and it had so many flaws from the start that when we reintroduced it we should have called it the Apple IV."**
>
> **Steve Wozniak**

Even after revising the Apple III, sales remained disappointing. Analysts estimate Apple sold 3,000 to 3,500 units a month, just one tenth the sales rate of the venerable Apple II. According to InfoCorp, a Santa Clara research firm, the Apple III had an installed base of only 75,000 units by December 1983, compared to 1.3 million Apple IIs.

"The Apple III is designed to have a 10-year lifespan."
Mike Markkula
The Wall Street Journal,
April 15, 1981, p. 29

Potential buyers had been turned off by all of the bad publicity as well as a lack of useful software that took advantage of the Apple III's unique Sophisticated Operating System. Industry experts openly referred to the operating system by its distress-signal initials, SOS, although Apple preferred the nickname "applesauce."

"Apple is firmly and totally committed to supporting the Apple III and is maintaining and increasing our commitment to the Apple III as a major product for the next five to seven years."

Mike Markkula
Computer Systems News,
November 16/23, 1981, p. 16

In a last-ditch effort to revive the product, Apple replaced the Apple III with the $2,995 Apple III Plus in December 1983. In addition to a lower price, the new model came standard with 256K of memory, a built-in clock that actually worked, a new logic board, SOS version 1.3, improved peripheral ports with standard DB-25 connectors, and a modified slot housing for easier card installation. Unfortunately, it was a classic case of too little, too late.

"The Apple III will be a serious contender in the business computer marketplace for a long time to come."

David Fradin
The Peninsula Times Tribune,
November 21, 1983, p. D4

Although the Apple III Plus had helped boost the installed base to an estimated 120,000 units, Apple abruptly
dropped the line on April 24, 1984. In a memo to his
staff, David Fradin, Apple III business unit manager, wrote
"While the Apple III is an excellent business computer, it
is a generally accepted view by Apple's product managers
that Apple can best serve the future needs of our business
computers by expanding the Apple II and Apple 32 [Lisa
and Mac] product families, and by concentrating future
development, marketing and sales efforts on these products. Therefore, we have decided that no further product
development efforts shall be initiated and undertaken for
the Apple III product line, effective immediately."

**"No further product development
efforts shall be initiated and
undertaken for the Apple III
product line, effective
immediately."**

David Fradin
internal memo, April 24,
1984

After losing over $60 million on the Apple
III, it was quietly removed from Apple's
product list in September 1985.

Millionaire Mania

Getting a company off the ground always requires sacrifices, and in that regard Apple was no different than any other. To scrape together the cost of producing the original Apple I printed circuit board in 1976, Steve Jobs parted with his red & white Volkswagen bus for $1,500 and Steve Wozniak sold his beloved Hewlett-Packard 65 programmable calculator for $250. The company was hobbling along when retired businessman Mike Markkula poured $92,000 into Apple's coffers.

The time and money each sacrificed to make Apple a success were amply rewarded on December 12, 1980 when the company went public. Apple Computer sold 4.6 million shares of stock at an initial public offering (IPO) price of $22, and the stock rose almost 32 percent

Courtesy of Volkswagon United States and Hewlett-Packard Co.

Jobs and Woz sold a VW bus and HP calculator, respectively, to finance the Apple I.

37

that day to close at $29. Jobs, the single largest stock-holder with 7.5 million shares, suddenly had a net worth exceeding $217 million. Not too shabby for a college drop-out. Woz's 4 million shares were worth a respectable $116 million. Pretty good for a wire-head who never wanted to build a company. Even Markkula couldn't complain. His 7 million shares were valued at $203 million, for an unbelievable 55,943 percent annualized return on his original 1977 stake!

The three founders of Apple Computer weren't the only ones who did well that fateful day in December. More than 40 other Apple employees became instant million-aires thanks to their stock options. (An option is a form of compensation which grants an employee the right to purchase stock at a specified exercise price.) Stock op-tions are a way of life in Silicon Valley, and in the late 1970s Apple routinely enticed candidates for employ-ment with options on a few thousand shares of stock with exercise prices of roughly $4.

Each share of stock issued prior to April 1979 was known as a "founder's share." Thanks to a series of five stock splits prior to the IPO, each founder's share multiplied into 32 shares with an average exercise price of 12.5¢. So anyone who owned a little over 1,000 founder's shares went to bed a millionaire on December 12, 1980.

But not everyone who helped build Apple was richly rewarded. Stock options were reserved for salaried employees such as engineers, not hourly employees such as technicians. Many of Apple's earliest employees were either too inexperienced or too naive to demand stock options. Let's face it, many of them were just teenagers and college kids like Jobs. A telling example is Daniel G. Kottke,

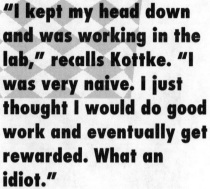

"I kept my head down and was working in the lab," recalls Kottke. "I was very naive. I just thought I would do good work and eventually get rewarded. What an idiot."

who had been Jobs' best friend at Reed College and who traveled to India with him seeking spiritual enlightenment.

Originally called in to help stuff Apple I circuit boards in 1976, Kottke became employee #12 in June, 1977, and was paid minimum wage to assemble and test Apple II motherboards. By 1980, Kottke was doing much more demanding work, building and troubleshooting the Apple III prototype, but he remained an hourly technician.

Kottke wanted the title of engineer more than the options which went with the position, but he wasn't a complete idiot. "I wanted to invest in the company. I had been working there since it started and I wasn't intending to leave. I deserved to invest," says Kottke, who at the time was sharing a house in Cupertino with Jobs and Jobs' former girlfriend who would later bear his child, Lisa.

Courtesy of Dan Kottke

Dan Kottke displaying the Apple I with Steve Jobs at the PC-76 show in Atlantic City, New Jersey in 1976.

Rod Holt, engineering vice president, was so uncomfortable with the inequity of the situation that he personally approached Jobs and suggested that they both give Kottke some stock by matching each other's contribution. Jobs reportedly exclaimed, "Great! I'll give him zero."

> **"I kept asking Steve about stock options and he would always put me off, saying that I had to talk to my supervisors. I found out a couple of years later that Jobs was the head of the Compensation Committee in charge of distributing options."**
>
> **Dan Kottke**

Even though his "best friend" was unwilling to grant him any options, Kottke eventually managed to get some shares. Holt unilaterally gave Kottke 100 shares out of his own pocket, and just before Apple went public, Kottke went to chairman Markkula and president Mike Scott and explained how unhappy he was because he hadn't gotten any shares. "I told them that I was going to leave the company," recalls Kottke. "They gave me options on 1,000 shares at around $8, but it was too late" for the stock splits which made others fabulously wealthy.

"A person like him shouldn't have that much money."

Jerry Wozniak,
Steve Wozniak's father, after finding $250,000 worth of uncashed checks strewn about his son Steve's car.
The Little Kingdom, p.282

Kottke's allotment was augmented through the generosity of Steve Wozniak, who felt that it was unfair that many of the earliest Apple employees—including Chris Espinosa, Bill Fernandez, and Randy Wigginton—failed to get stock options.

Working on the WozPlan

In 1980, Woz was about to sell $2 million worth of stock to buy a house and get a car. He had an outside buyer lined up to buy the stock and the two had agreed upon what they considered to be a fair price even though it was pretty obvious that the stock was going to be worth a lot more when Apple went public. "I had an offer from a qualified buyer, so I just thought I'll sell it at that price to Apple employees," says Woz. So he set up a program called the WozPlan that allowed certain employees to buy up to 2,000 shares each.

Initially the lawyers in the company had a problem with Woz selling to "unqualified buyers," because they didn't want to upset the Securities and Exchange Commission prior to the IPO, but eventually when the details of the plan were made clear, chief counsel Al Eisenstat gave the OK. In the end, about 80 people participated in the WozPlan, with some buying shares at a very advantageous price, and a select few receiving outright gifts of a substantial number of shares.

Even though Jobs remarked that "Woz ended up giving stock to all the wrong people," Wozniak takes great pleasure from his good deed. "Over the years, a lot of people have called to thank me for making it possible for them to do things—buy houses, send kids to college, etc.—that they otherwise would never have been able to afford. That makes it all worthwhile."

"People think I'm an asshole, don't they?"

Steve Jobs
The Big Score, p.366

"I had much more money than I could ever dream of, and I felt that everyone who had participated in engineering and marketing should be part owners of the company," recalls Woz. "A few of us were going to be making a huge amount of money, yet the others weren't really valued. Mike Markkula's opinion was that these people weren't worthy and weren't entitled to stock. Only the managers with the right college backgrounds who were hired above them got the stock options and were going to make a lot of money. I just wanted to help the others because they were important, too."

Taking Stock of Apple

Apple Computer stock trades in the over the counter (OTC) market and is listed on NASDAQ under the symbol AAPL, on the Tokyo Stock Exchange under the symbol APPLE, and on the Frankfurt Stock Exchange under the symbol APCD.

"[Jobs] originally believed that the company could sell five million Macintoshes in the first two years. That's such a crazy number that it's ridiculous. No one has ever done that with any machine."

Trip Hawkins,
former manager
of marketing
planning at Apple
Accidental Millionaire,
p. 144

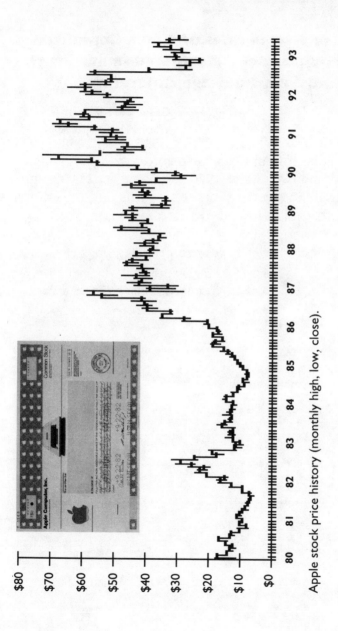

Apple stock price history (monthly high, low, close).

"Long-term sales of Apple Computer products depends upon dominating the minds of school-age children."

Gene Carter, former
VP of marketing at Apple

Apple's first formal business plan drawn up by Mike Markkula in November 1976 set a goal for sales to grow to $500 million in ten years. As it turns out, the company passed that mark in half the time.

In May 1983, Apple entered the Fortune 500 at number 411—in under five years, the fastest ascent in business history.

IBM: The Strangest Bedfellow of All

In the late 1970s, Apple was the standout in the crowded personal computer field. The Apple II sold briskly into the home and education markets, and had even made headway into business offices thanks to the popularity of VisiCalc. The entire personal computer industry was enjoying phenomenal growth, and Apple was leading the pack. But Apple knew it was only a matter of time before it faced the most formidable competitor of all, International Business Machines of Armonk, New York. The day of reckoning arrived on August 12, 1981, when IBM introduced its $1,565 personal computer with a single 5.25-inch floppy disk drive and 16 kilobytes of memory.

Courtesy of Apple Computer, Inc.

Mike Markkula

47

"We've been planning and waiting for IBM to get into the marketplace for four years. We're the guys in the driver's seat. We're the guys with one third of a million installed base. We're the guys with a software library. We're the guys with distribution. It's IBM who is reacting and responding to Apple. They'll have to do a lot more reacting and responding. IBM hasn't the foggiest notion of how to sell to individuals. It took us four years to learn about it. They must learn about distribution structure and independent dealers. You cannot reduce time by throwing money at it. Short of World War III nothing is going to knock us out of the box."

Mike Markkula,
then Apple president
The Little Kingdom, p. 310

"We're going to out-market IBM. We've got our shit together."

Steve Jobs, then Apple
chairman
Accidental Millionaire, p. 148

Jean-Louis Gassée

"From the standpoint of Apple, the existence of IBM on the personal computer market has been very profitable. First, because it made us come down to earth by putting things in perspective and restoring competition. Second, because Big Blue lent an air of respectability to a product that, not so long ago, was considered marginal and superfluous."

Jean-Louis Gassée, former president of Apple Products
The Third Apple, p. 81

Courtesy of Xerox Corp. and Brian Tramontana of Xerox PARC

Alan Kay

"The IBM PC is beneath comment. It's been known for 12 years how to do a good-looking display and IBM didn't put one on its machine. You can't have any favorable comment beyond that. That is the ultimate in know-nothingness."

Alan Kay, Apple Fellow
InfoWorld, June 11, 1984,
p. 59

> **"It's curious to me that the largest computer company in the world [IBM] couldn't even match the Apple II, which was designed in a garage six years ago, after studying it. It is interesting."**

Steve Jobs
InfoWorld, March 8, 1982

Welcome, IBM.

Seriously.

Welcome to the most exciting and important marketplace since the computer revolution began 35 years ago.

And congratulations on your first personal computer.

Putting real computer power in the hands of the individual is already improving the way people work, think, learn, communicate and spend their leisure hours.

Computer literacy is fast becoming as fundamental a skill as reading or writing.

When we invented the first personal computer system, we estimated that over 140,000,000 people worldwide could justify the purchase of one, if only they understood its benefits.

Next year alone, we project that well over 1,000,000 will come to that understanding. Over the next decade, the growth of the personal computer will continue in logarithmic leaps.

We look forward to responsible competition in the massive effort to distribute this American technology to the world. And we appreciate the magnitude of your commitment.

Because what we are doing is increasing social capital by enhancing individual productivity.

Welcome to the task. **apple**

Courtesy of BBDO, and Apple Computer, Inc.

On August 24, Apple responded to IBM's introduction in an amazing display of bravado by placing a full page advertisement in The *Wall Street Journal* welcoming the pin-striped corporate behemoth into the market that Apple practically saw as its birthright. While Apple clearly viewed the IBM PC as second-rate technology, the buying public didn't look much farther than those magical initials which represented stability, service, and reliability. To them, it didn't much matter what was inside the box, the IBM PC was a serious business machine from a serious company, and it didn't take long for Apple to realize it was in serious trouble. By the end of the year, IBM had sold 50,000 computers, and after two years passed Apple in dollar sales of the machines.

In 1983, Apple's market share of personal computers edged up from 20% to 21%, while IBM's rose dramatically from 18% to 26%, according to Future Computing, a Texas-based consulting firm.

"As it turned out, the original welcome was like Little Red Ridinghood's welcoming the wolf into her grandmother's home. There is a very fine line between being self-confident and getting cocky about it."

John Sculley
Playboy, September 1987, p. 58

Apple tried to stem the tide with the January 1983 introduction of the Lisa. By all accounts, the Lisa was a revolutionary computer, but as far as the business community was concerned, it had two major flaws. First, its $9,995 price tag was too expensive. Second, and perhaps most importantly, it wasn't compatible with anything else on the market. The IBM PC and Microsoft's MS-DOS had established a standard to which clone manufacturers flocked, but Apple resisted the temptation to go with the flow. Right or wrong, Apple has always felt that its technology was better, if not the best, and if it just waited long enough, the world would recognize this fact and be willing to pay a premium to buy a computer from Cupertino.

> "It would be easy for us to come out with an IBM look-alike product, and put the Apple logo on it, and sell a lot of Apples. Our earnings per share would go up and our stockholders would be happy, but we think that would be the wrong thing to do."
>
> **John Sculley**, then Apple president and CEO
>
> *Fortune*, February 20, 1984, p. 94

53

"We're not going to sell five million [Macs] a year by being IBM compatible. We're going to do it by making a second industry standard."

Steve Jobs
Fortune, February 20, 1984, p. 98

"I think they'll make refrigerators first."

Aaron Goldberg, computer market researcher for International Data Corporation, when asked if Apple will ever offer an IBM-compatible product
Fortune, February 20, 1984, p. 98

On February 28, 1994, Apple began shipping the Macintosh Quadra 610 DOS Compatible, a full-featured personal computer with MS-DOS- and Windows-compatibility. Apparently the two-door, frost-free model with built-in ice maker is currently undergoing beta testing in select kitchens across America.

By 1984, it was clear that the Lisa was a sales disappointment, and industry pundits were decrying the Apple II as dated technology destined to die any day now (a flawed assessment "experts" would repeat many times over the decade). Apple desperately needed a hit to combat IBM, and Steve Jobs had made up his mind to bet everything on the Macintosh. Part of his strategy was to get the public thinking of Apple versus IBM in terms of a two-horse race like Coke and Pepsi, Hertz and Avis, *Time* and *Newsweek*. Never was this strategy executed as effectively as in the landmark *1984* commercial which heralded the introduction of the Macintosh on January 24, 1984.

"It really is coming down to just Apple and IBM. If, for some reason, we make some giant mistake and IBM wins, my personal feeling is that we are going to enter sort of a computer Dark Ages for about 20 years."

Steve Jobs
Playboy, February 1985, p. 70

"IBM wants to wipe us off the face of the earth."

Steve Jobs
Fortune, February 20, 1984

55

Throughout the 1980s, Apple tenaciously fought to maintain its modest market share against encroachment from IBM and the many clone makers, but after enjoying years of beefy profit margins, price wars late in the decade had slashed hardware margins to the bone. While mulling over Apple's predicament, John Sculley had an epiphany when he finally came to accept what many people had been saying all along: Apple's real strength isn't hardware, it's software, specifically, the Mac's easy-to-use operating system. Therefore, Apple's real enemy isn't IBM, but rather, Microsoft. In an about-face that shocked the industry, Apple decided to join forces with its old adversary in Armonk to take on its new nemesis to the north.

On April 12, 1991, Sculley gave a hush-hush demonstration to a group of IBM's top engineers. They saw Apple's secret object-oriented operating system (code-named Pink) running on an IBM PS/2 Model 70, making it look and feel a lot like a Mac running System 7! Impressed, IBM signed a letter of intent with Apple on July 3, 1991, pledging to help finish Pink and give Apple a license to its reduced instruction set computer (RISC) processor, the PowerPC.

> **"We want to be a major player in the computer industry, not a niche player. The only way to do that is to work with another major player."**
>
> **John Sculley**

On October 2, 1991, the historic alliance became official when Apple and IBM signed the papers during a press conference at the Fairmont Hotel in San Francisco. The two former enemies agreed to work on computers based upon the PowerPC chip manufactured by Motorola, and established two spin-off companies called Taligent and Kaleida. Taligent would complete Pink, and Kaleida was to create multimedia tools.

Courtesy of Apple Computer, Inc.

IBM's Jack Kuehler and Apple's John Sculley proudly presenting their "marriage certificate" in October 1991.

Some speculate that IBM was simply hedging its bets against the possibility of Apple winning its 1988 "look and feel" lawsuit against Microsoft and then coming after IBM for Presentation Manager, which is similar to Windows. As it happened, Apple's suit started heading south at just about the same time the company got into bed with IBM, and was eventually dismissed in 1993.

Q. What do you get when you cross Apple and IBM?

A. IBM

It's too early to tell how history will remember the famous Apple-IBM pact of 1991. Apple's Power Macintoshes, based upon the first-generation PowerPC 601 from Motorola, were introduced on March 14, 1994 and have garnered favorable reviews for their unbeatable price/performance ratios and excellent compatibility with existing Macintosh software and hardware. Rumor has it that Taligent's Pink operating system is hopelessly behind schedule, and Kaleida was forced to lay off 20 percent of its work force on May 9, 1994 due to financial cut-backs. Stay tuned...

"[PowerPC supporters] are smoking dope. There's no way it's going to work."

> **Robert W. Stearns,** VP of corporate development at Compaq Computers

Lisa: From Xerox with Love

Putting the Macintosh into proper historical perspective is impossible without considering its forerunner, Apple's ill-fated Lisa computer. The Lisa began life in the fall of 1978 when Steve Jobs and William "Trip" Hawkins III (manager of marketing planning) began brainstorming about a next-generation project that would break from the Apple II mold, but it wasn't until July 30, 1979 that the Lisa project really got under way when Ken Rothmuller was hired as project manager. As originally conceived, the Lisa was nothing like the Macintosh. For that matter, Lisa, the project, bore little resemblance to Lisa, the product.

In 1979, Lisa existed only as a set of specifications calling for a $2,000 business computer to ship in March 1981 with a built-in green phosphor display, keyboard, and rather traditional user interface. The basic idea of designing the computer around a bit-slice microprocessor was discarded when it became apparent that would be far too expensive. As it turned out, hardly anything from the original plan made it into the shipping product beside the name. What caused Apple to radically change the Lisa? In a word: Xerox.

Courtesy of Xerox Corp. and Brian Tramontana of Xerox PARC

Xerox Palo Alto Research Center, birthplace of many computing firsts.

Anxious to be on the cutting-edge of information technology, in 1970 the Xerox Corporation gathered many of the best minds in the computer industry and ensconced them in the Palo Alto Research Center (PARC) at 3333 Coyote Hill Road in Palo Alto, California. Their mission was to create the future, without worrying about the practicality of actually marketing their creations as commercial products.

By 1973, they had succeeded in giving birth to the Xerox Alto, the embodiment of many computing firsts. It was the first personal computer in the sense that it was designed to be used by a single person. Rather than putting fully-formed characters on screen one at a time, the Alto created both text and graphics out of individually-controlled pixels using a process called bit-mapping. Using Ethernet, another PARC creation, the Alto could network with other Alto computers and laser printers,

yet another PARC invention. It had an object-oriented programming language—Smalltalk—with reusable, self-contained modules of code. And it featured a funny pointing device, a three-button mouse.

The Alto was a revolutionary creation, but it wasn't a product. If it had been sold commercially with the industry's customary gross margins, it might have cost as much as $40,000.

Many Lisa features were borrowed from the Xerox Alto.

Courtesy of Xerox Corp. and Brian Tramontana of Xerox PARC

Even though the Alto was never sold to the public, it was well known in Silicon Valley. The PARC researchers were proud of their creations and willingly showed them off to many curious visitors who dropped by the campus during the early years. One person in particular who had been impressed with their work was Jef Raskin, an Apple employee who was heading up a small, obscure research project code-named Macintosh. As a visiting scholar at the Stanford Artificial Intelligence Laboratory in the early 1970s, Raskin spent a lot of time at PARC and thought what they were doing there was wonderful.

> **"The original Lisa was a character-generator machine. I spent days with the Lisa team trying to explain that it could be done all in graphics, like the Alto. In that regard, I had a very strong influence on the Lisa; I was trying to make it more like the Mac. I thought they were headed in the wrong direction."**
>
> **Jef Raskin**

Raskin tried convincing Jobs that he should go see the wonderful stuff at Xerox PARC, but in his binary way of viewing the world, Jobs then considered Raskin a "shithead who could do no good," so he ignored his recommendation. But Raskin had an ally in software engineer Bill Atkinson, who had been his student at the University of California at San Diego and now worked on LisaGraf primatives, the basic graphics routines of the Lisa (ultimately these would be named QuickDraw, a term Raskin

coined in his 1967 Penn State thesis). In Jobs' eyes, Atkinson was a hero who could do no wrong, so when Atkinson pushed Jobs to visit Xerox PARC, Jobs agreed. But by then, Xerox had tightened security at the facility. Fortunately, Jobs had just what it took to open the doors.

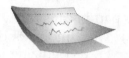

Jobs approached the Xerox Development Corporation, the venture capital branch of the copier giant, and boldly told them "I will let you invest a million dollars in Apple if you will sort of open the kimono at Xerox PARC."

At the time, Apple was enjoying meteoric growth and was in the midst of its second private investment placement. Xerox was anxious to get a piece of the action and was more than willing to allow an Apple contingent to take a peek at PARC. After all, an investment in Apple was likely to turn a handsome profit when the company eventually went public, whereas the stuff languishing in the PARC labs was an intangible asset that might very well never make it to market. Xerox signed an agreement never to purchase more than five percent of Apple's shares and invested $1 million by buying 100,000 shares at $10 each (within a year these split into 800,000 shares worth $17.6 million when Apple went public).

In return, Apple was allowed two afternoon visits to the PARC labs. When Jobs first visited with Atkinson in November 1979, he saw with his own eyes what all the fuss was about. He was so excited that he returned in December with Hawkins, Rothmuller, Richard Page (hardware engineer), John Dennis Couch (VP of software), Michael M. Scott (president), Dr. Thomas M.

Whitney (executive VP of engineering), and Bruce Daniels (software engineer). Xerox researcher Lawrence G. Tesler had planned to give the Apple group the same dog-and-pony Smalltalk show that Xerox had put on many times before, but it didn't take long for Tesler to realize that the guys from Apple were different.

They "got it" immediately, in large part because they had been extensively briefed by Raskin. They understood the importance of what they were shown, recognizing the subtle details that made it better than everything else. They asked all the right questions. Jobs began jumping around, shouting, "Why aren't you doing anything with this? This is the greatest thing! This is revolutionary!"

Courtesy of Apple Computer, Inc.

Alan Kay

"We had very few visitors who were multiple-hundred-dollar millionaires, in their twenties, and heads of companies, so most of the people who visited were not able to simply go back and, by fiat, say this is what we want."

Alan Kay, former Xerox researcher, explaining why Jobs' PARC visit was different from the many others

A History of Personal Workstations, pp. 343-344

If Xerox didn't recognize the value of its own employees' work, Jobs certainly did. When he saw the Alto running Smalltalk with its overlapping windows, miniature icons, and pop-up menus, he knew that's what he wanted and he instructed the Lisa crew to begin working in that direction. It's easy to say that Apple stole the Alto from Xerox and marketed it as the Lisa, but that shortchanges the brilliance and hard work of the Lisa team. Apple didn't get blueprints from Xerox, but rather inspiration. "Just like the Russians and the A-bomb," observed PARC's director, George Pake. "They developed it very quickly once they knew it was doable." (*Fumbling the Future*, p. 242)

In December 1989, Xerox filed a suit challenging the validity of Apple's copyrights covering the Lisa and Mac graphic user interfaces. In March 1990, the court dismissed most of the lawsuit.

Actually, development of the Lisa didn't go so quickly or smoothly, even after the PARC visit. Jobs was trying to distance himself from the Apple III which he helped botch, so he began meddling with the Lisa project, arguing over almost every design decision. Nonetheless, by March 1980, Hawkins had completed a marketing requirements document that specified a graphical user interface, mouse, local area network, file servers, and innovative software applications. After complaining that there was no way they could incorporate all these features and stick to the original schedule and $2,000 target, Rothmuller was fired for being uncooperative (of course, he would be proven correct in due time). During the summer, Tesler left Xerox and joined Apple to work with Atkinson defining the ground rules of the Lisa's user interface. Eventually more than 15 Xerox employees would join Apple, including Bob Belleville, Steve Capps, Alan Kay, and Barbara Koalkin.

"Steve had an incredible ability to rally people towards some common cause by painting an incredibly glorious cosmic objective. One of his favorite statements about the Lisa was, 'Let's make a dent in the universe. We'll make it so important that it will make a dent in the universe.'"

Trip Hawkins
The Journey Is the Reward,
p. 187

Courtesy of The 3DO Company

Trip Hawkins

Just as the Lisa project was coming into focus, Scott reorganized Apple along product lines in the fall of 1980. Jobs desperately wanted control of the high-visibility Lisa project, which was now part of the Personal Office Systems (POS) division, but Scott was no fool. He knew firsthand that Jobs was an extremely combative manager who lacked technical expertise, a fact that was becoming painfully apparent as the Apple III floundered due to some of Jobs' design mandates. There was no way Scott was going to put Jobs in charge of a project as important as Lisa. Instead, Scott named John Couch as VP and general manager of POS and tried to soften the blow to Jobs by asking him to act as the corporate spokesman as Apple prepared for its initial public offering which would take place that December. Jobs, the consummate showman and media darling, was born for the role, but he would never forgive Scott for denying him the opportunity to bring Lisa to market.

Even with Jobs out of the way, the Lisa was slow to market because the Lisa team refused to simply churn out an Appleized Alto. Sure, it borrowed pop-up menus and overlapping windows from Smalltalk, but it also invented the concepts of the menu bar, pull-down menus, scroll bars, the one-button mouse, cutting and pasting with the Clipboard, and the Trash can.

One major advance came relatively late in the game. After studying the $16,595 Xerox Star (a variation on the Alto) at the June 1981 National Computer Conference in Houston, a small band of Lisa software engineers led by Atkinson decided to make some fundamental changes to the operating system's user interface, resulting in icons that you can drag and double-click to open. Everything fell into place nicely after that. On July 30, 1982, the Lisa team managed to get its entire collection of applications to function together for the first time. By September 1, the Lisa was officially declared ready for market, so the following months were devoted to squashing the long list of known bugs.

> **"We're going to blow IBM away. There's nothing they can do when this computer comes out. This is so revolutionary, it's incredible."**
>
> **Steve Jobs,** describing the Lisa to John Sculley
>
> *Odyssey,* p. 69

> **"We want to drive this industry. We could have introduced Lisa a year ago, but we wanted to make it perfect. We're prepared to live with Lisa for the next ten years."**
>
> **Steve Jobs**
>
> *Time*, January 31, 1983, p. 51

Courtesy of Apple Computer, Inc.

While innovative, the Lisa was expensive and sold poorly.

After more than 200 person-years of hard work (by way of comparison, the Apple II required only two person-years to complete) and $50 million in development costs, the Lisa was formally introduced on January 19, 1983 during Apple's annual stockholders' meeting at De Anza College's Flint Center in Cupertino (the Apple IIe was introduced simultaneously under the theme "Evolution and Revolution").

The Lisa weighed 48 pounds and featured a Motorola 68000 microprocessor running at 5 megahertz, 1 megabyte of random access memory, two 5.25-inch 860-kilobyte floppy disk drives, a 5-megabyte hard disk (the same

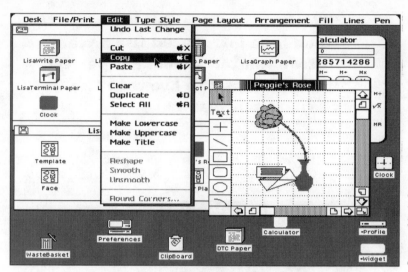

Courtesy of Apple Computer, Inc.

ProFile originally designed for the Apple III), detachable keyboard, one-button mouse, and built-in 12-inch, bit-mapped monochrome display of 720 by 364 pixels.

Since it was incompatible with everything else on the market, the Lisa was bundled with seven applications: a spreadsheet, draw program, graphing program,

"We're really banking everything on Lisa's technology. If Lisa fails, we'll be just another half-billion or billion-dollar computer company."

Steve Jobs, carefully specifying Lisa technology, not the Lisa itself

Business Week, January 31, 1983, p. 70

file manager, project manager, terminal emulator, and word processor. The Lisa came with everything, including a list price of $9,995. As Rothmuller had warned, feature creep boosted the price of the computer to the point where only well-heeled businesses could afford it. Instead of its traditional personal computer competitors Atari, Commodore, and Radio Shack, Apple found itself going up against the big guns of DEC, IBM, Wang, and Xerox.

"Lisa is going to be incredibly great. It will sell twelve thousand units in the first six months and fifty thousand in the first year."

Steve Jobs,
seriously over-
estimating
demand
The Little Kingdom, p. 16

According to InfoCorp, Apple sold only 60,000 Lisas over its two-year lifespan.

Formidable competition wasn't the only factor inhibiting Lisa's market acceptance. In large measure, Apple con-tributed to its own undoing. First there was that list price just shy of $10,000. Apple simply had no experience sell-ing computers at that price point, so it had to build an elitist, 100-person sales staff from the ground up. Then there was all that bundled software. Giving the customer everything they could possibly need must have seemed like a good idea at the time, but it stifled third-party development efforts. Also, the Lisa was so slow that it inspired a popular "Knock Knock" joke wherein the response to "Who's there?" was a fifteen-second pause followed by the word "Lisa."

If all that wasn't bad enough, Apple was also bedeviled by the Lisa's floppy disk drives which Jobs stubbornly insisted on developing in-house. The Apple 871 disk drive—code-named Twiggy after the 1960s "mod" British fashion model because both were thin—provided a whopping amount of storage, but was notoriously unreliable. Finally, and perhaps most damaging, even before the Lisa began shipping in June, the press was full of intentionally-leaked rumors about a fall release of a "baby Lisa" that would work in much the same way, only faster and cheaper. Its name: Macintosh.

The revamped Lisa 2 was introduced along with the Macintosh.

Courtesy of Apple Computer, Inc.

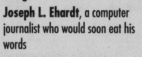

"Whatever Apple's plans are, we think it extremely unlikely that it would introduce a similar product that would undercut their Lisa system so soon after its costly development and introduction. Indeed, we cannot see the benefit that would be gained by such action. So, whatever MacIntosh [sic] may turn out to be and whenever it finally appears, we think it is more likely that it will be clearly differentiated from the Lisa offering."

Joseph L. Ehardt, a computer journalist who would soon eat his words

The Seybold Report on Professional Computing, January 28, 1983, p. 25

Apple recognized some of its mistakes, and on September 12, 1983, it unbundled the suite of software and began selling the Lisa hardware at reduced price of $6,995. Then on January 24, 1984, when Apple introduced the Macintosh, it also announced the revamped Lisa 2 series. The base model now cost $3,495, had half the memory of the original, twice the speed, and a robust 3.5-inch, 400K Sony disk drive borrowed from the Mac; the high-end model, the Lisa 2/10, had more memory and a 10MB hard disk drive.

Lisa sales began picking up as the Mac pulled people into dealer showrooms and many realized they needed more than the Mac offered. Still, Apple shipped three times as many Macs in its first 100 days than Lisas in its first year. In an attempt to consolidate the product line in

Lisa Timeline

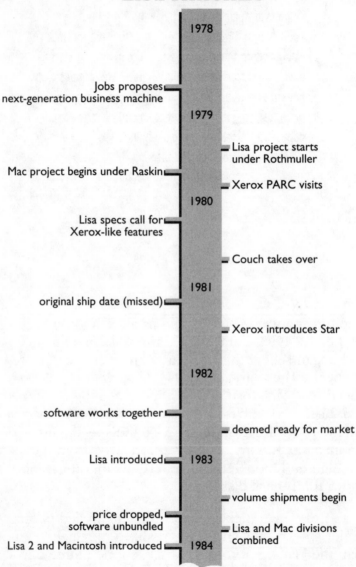

1978

Jobs proposes
next-generation business machine

1979

Lisa project starts
under Rothmuller

Mac project begins under Raskin

Xerox PARC visits

1980

Lisa specs call for
Xerox-like features

Couch takes over

1981

original ship date (missed)

Xerox introduces Star

1982

software works together

deemed ready for market

Lisa introduced   1983

volume shipments begin

price dropped,
software unbundled

Lisa and Mac divisions
combined

Lisa 2 and Macintosh introduced   1984

Lisa Timeline

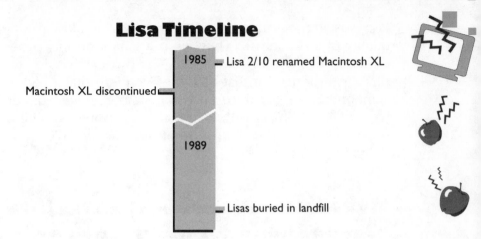

1985 — Lisa 2/10 renamed Macintosh XL

Macintosh XL discontinued

1989

Lisas buried in landfill

January 1985, Apple changed the name of the Lisa 2/10 to Macintosh XL, dropped the other Lisa models, and introduced MacWorks, an emulation program that allowed Lisa to run Mac software. The renamed Lisa began holding its own, but ironically it would soon be killed by the very man who once brought it to life: Steve Jobs.

A lot had happened since Scott denied Jobs the chance to head the Lisa project in 1980. In March 1981, Mike Markkula took over the presidency from Scott, and Jobs succeeded Markkula as chairman. In April 1983, Jobs convinced John Sculley to leave Pepsi-Cola to become president and CEO of Apple. Impressed by his young suitor, Sculley gave Jobs free reign over the Macintosh division, and in November, the Lisa and Mac divisions were combined into the Apple 32 SuperMicro division with Jobs at the helm. His power thus consolidated, Jobs decided to put the newly renamed Lisa out of its misery.

By Sculley's own account, "Steve and several members of the Macintosh team believed the original design of the

75

Lisa wasn't good enough and that it never would have the quality of a Macintosh. They felt it wasn't a priority product and wanted it phased out. We obviously couldn't phase a product out that had just been introduced. So someone in the Macintosh division simply neglected, perhaps deliberately, to order parts and components to allow us to continue the manufacture of the Macintosh XL." (*Odyssey*, p. 240)

"We had to abandon [the Lisa] without honor or glory since we failed to raise sales to an adequate profit margin at a time when market growth was slowing down. All of which proves that it is difficult to revive a product that has made a poor start."

Jean-Louis
Gassée, former
president of
Apple Products
The Third Apple, p. 103

Apple officially discontinued the Macintosh XL, née Lisa, on April 29, 1985, and the last Lisa rolled off the assembly line at the Carrollton, Texas factory on May 15, 1985. Sun Remarketing of Logan, Utah purchased the 5,000 unsold Lisas in inventory and took several thousand more used and broken units on consignment. It did quite well selling

Courtesy of Be Inc.

Jean-Louis Gassée

the Lisas after upgrading them with the latest Mac technology, but in mid-September 1989, Apple decided to literally bury the Lisa once and for all. Under the watchful eyes of armed security guards, 2,700 Lisas that had been on consignment were interred at the Logan landfill (880 cubic yards at $1.95 a yard) so that Apple could receive a tax write-off.

"You guys really fucked up. I'm going to have to lay a lot of you off."

Steve Jobs, to the Lisa troops, after consolidating the Lisa and Mac divisions

The Journey Is the Reward, p. 339-340

> "It [Lisa] was a great machine. We just couldn't sell any."
>
> **Bruce Tognazzini**, former
> human interface guru at Apple
> *Accidental Millionaire*, p. 174

Courtesy of Kevin Rice

The last of the Lisas in the Logan landfill.

Code Name Confusion

Like the Macintosh, the ill-fated Lisa made it to market with its code name intact. There are many conflicting rumors about the origin of the name. The most widely circulated story is that the Lisa was named after Steve Jobs' daughter who was born out of wedlock. This much we know as fact: On June 17, 1978, Jobs' high school sweetheart and former live-in girlfriend gave birth to a little girl in Oregon, whom the 23-year-old Jobs helped name Lisa Nicole. In 1979, a paternity suit was filed against Jobs. Even after a blood test performed by the University of California reported that the probability of Jobs being Lisa's father was 94.4 percent, Jobs dismissed the possibility. Nonetheless, he didn't want the suit dragging on—after all, Apple would soon go public, making him exceedingly rich—so he agreed to pay child support of $385 a month, provide health insurance for Lisa, and reimburse public assistance for the baby in the amount of $5,856. (Jobs eventually came to accept Lisa as his daughter and today the two are often spotted together in Palo Alto, where Jobs lives at 2101 Waverly Street.)

Was the Lisa named for Jobs' daughter? The project began several months after the birth of Lisa Nicole, so the timing is right. Also, during this period at Apple, it was customary to name projects after daughters of project leaders. While many therefore believe that the Lisa must have been named after Jobs' daughter, Steve Wozniak disagrees. "I know for a fact that Lisa was not named for Steve Jobs' illegitimate daughter," insists Woz. "It's not the truth. John Couch headed the Lisa program and he told me it was named after Ken Rothmuller's daughter, another key person behind the Lisa." Sadly, Rothmuller's only daughter is named Cheryl, and as he put it, "Jobs is such an egomaniac, do you really think he would have allowed such an important project to be named after anybody but his own child?"

No matter who the computer was named after, Apple figured it needed a more professional-sounding name to appeal to the business market, so it hired an outside consulting firm to recommend a new name. Among others, they suggested Applause, Apple IV, Apple 400, The Coach, Esprit, Teacher, and The World. Quite an effort went into thinking up a different name, but the forthcoming computer had already received so much press coverage under its code name that Trip Hawkins (who would later found Electronic Arts and The3DO Company) reverse engineered the explanation that Lisa stood for "Local Integrated Software Architecture." This was so obviously contrived that industry wags suggested a more accurate explanation was that Lisa stood for "Let's Invent Some Acronym."

In honor of John Sculley's previous employer, the Lisa 2 was code-named Pepsi before being renamed the Macintosh XL. While XL was supposed to convey the impression of an extra large Macintosh, insiders joked that it really stood for "eX-Lisa" or "eXtra Lisas" in inventory.

Folon's Forgotten Logo

When you turn on any Mac, the first thing you see (unless you have a customized StartupScreen in your System folder) is the familiar "Welcome to Macintosh" greeting beside a Picasso-inspired drawing of the original Mac. That little drawing is so universally known as the artistic representation of the soul of the Macintosh that it's difficult to imagine any other image evoking the same response. Therefore it may surprise you to learn that it was not what Apple had originally planned.

This lovable little Mac logo wasn't what Jobs originally wanted.

81

> "[Jobs] has the ability to make people around him believe in his perception of reality. It's a combination of very fast comeback, catch phrases, and the occasional, very original insight, which he throws in to keep you off balance."
>
> **Bud Tribble**, former manager of Mac software engineering
> *The Journey Is the Reward*, p. 206

Long before the Mac was complete, Steve Jobs had become quite taken with the work of Belgian-born poster artist Jean-Michel Folon, and paid him an advance of $30,000 to design a logo to represent the new computer. Folon came up with a character he called Mac Man and depicted him in a color pastel drawing called The Macintosh Spirit.

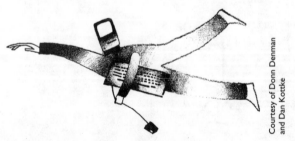

Courtesy of Donn Denman and Dan Kottke

Jobs passed on Folon's Macintosh Spirit.

In addition to his hefty advance, Folon was to be paid an unbelievable royalty of $1 for every Mac sold, but after he submitted The Macintosh Spirit, the mercurial Jobs changed his mind. He turned instead to the Mac art director, Tom Hughes, asking him to come up with something a little more practical. Working with John Casado, Hughes created the colorful, simple drawing of the Mac that we've come to know and love.

To make ends meet in the summer of 1972, Woz, Jobs, and Jobs' girlfriend took $3-per-hour jobs in the Westgate Mall in San Jose, California dressing up as *Alice In Wonderland* characters. Jobs and Woz alternated as the White Rabbit and the Mad Hatter. (*Accidental Millionaire*, p. 24)

The Making of Macintosh

Steve Jobs and the Macintosh are inextricably linked in the minds of most people. So it may come somewhat as a surprise to learn that the Mac wasn't his idea at all. In fact, he actually wanted to kill the project in its infancy. Lucky for Apple and millions of dedicated Mac users everywhere, he wasn't successful. The story of how the Mac came to be is a fascinating tale of one man's inspiration, another man's ego, and the dedication of a small band of "pirates" that forever changed the way the world computes.

In 1994, while Apple and all the major Macintosh publications were celebrating the Mac's 10th anniversary, one man was quietly celebrating its 15th. That man is Jef Raskin, the true father of the Macintosh. Raskin, a professor-turned-computer consultant, wrote the Integer BASIC manual for the Apple II in 1976. When he joined Apple on January 3, 1978 as employee #31, 34-year-old Raskin was manager of the Publications department. Over time he started a New Product Review division and an Application Software division.

In the spring of 1979, chairman Mike Markkula asked Raskin if he would work on a project code-named Annie, the goal of which was to produce a $500 game machine. At the time, Jobs and cohorts were working on the

business-oriented Lisa and the company felt it needed a lower-cost product than the Apple II, which was selling for well over $1,000 in a basic configuration without a disk drive or monitor.

Jef Raskin (center) with (from left to right) Michael Scott, Steve Jobs, Chris Espinosa, and Steve Wozniak.

"I told him it was a fine project, but I wasn't terribly interested in a game machine," remembers Raskin. "However, there was this thing that I'd been dreaming of for some time which I called Macintosh. The biggest thing about it was that it would be designed from a human factors perspective, which at that time was totally incomprehensible." Markkula was intrigued and asked Raskin to elaborate on his ideas and investigate the feasibility of putting them into practice.

Cold Cash for a Code Name

In naming his Macintosh project, Jef Raskin bucked the trend of using female code names. He thought the practice was sexist, and it was. The Annie project, for which Markkula originally tried to recruit Raskin, was a very thinly-veiled reference to Little Annie Fanny, the well-endowed cartoon character that regularly appeared in *Playboy* back then.

It's often reported that Raskin misspelled the name of his favorite variety of apples, but that's unlikely given that he was manager of publications. "I intentionally changed the spelling," explains Raskin. "I'm a pretty good speller. Writing is one of the things I do well. The name of the apple is McIntosh. I thought that would lead us to a conflict with McIntosh Laboratory, the hi-fi manufacturer. So I used the spelling Macintosh, figuring that if it conflicted with the overcoat, who cares?" Unfortunately, the slight spelling change wasn't enough to keep Apple in the clear.

When Apple attempted to trademark the name Macintosh in 1982, the request was denied because it phonetically infringed on the trademark already owned by an American manufacturer of audio equipment. McIntosh Laboratory of Binghamton, New York operates at the very high-end of the high-fidelity food chain, selling CD players for $2,000 and speakers that go from $1,600 to $25,000 a pair. On November 16, 1982, Steve Jobs wrote a letter to the president of McIntosh Labs, Gordon Gow, requesting a worldwide release for the name Macintosh. "We have become very attached to the name Macintosh. Much like one's own child, our product has developed a very definite personality," wrote Jobs.

Gow visited Cupertino shortly thereafter to take a look at what Apple was developing, but on the advice of his legal counsel, he rejected Jobs' request. Apple considered shortening Macintosh to MAC, which would stand for Mouse-Activated Computer outside the company, and Meaningless Acronym Computer internally. However, in late March 1983, Apple managed to license the rights to the name, and several years later purchased the trademark outright. Although the terms of these agreements remain confidential to this day, it has been reported that Apple paid $100,000 in cash for the Macintosh name. According to McIntosh's legal counsel, that's "substantially off the mark" and the real pay-off was "significantly higher."

"Throw thirty million dollars of advertising at it and it will sound great."

Ben Rosen, venture capitalist, when Jobs asked his opinion of the name Macintosh

The Little Kingdom, p. 18

By late May, Raskin had sketched out the basic ideas behind a computer for the "Person in the Street," known as the PITS, for short. Raskin had grown increasingly frustrated at the complexity of the Apple II. Its open architecture was good in the sense that you could fill its slots with anything you wanted, but that flexibility forced the user to be a pseudo-technician and made it extremely difficult for developers to create products that worked with all configurations.

"Considerations such as these led me to conceive the basic architecture and guiding principles of the Macintosh project. There were to be no peripheral slots so that customers never had to see the inside of the machine (although external ports would be provided); there was a fixed memory size so that all applications would run on all Macintoshes; the screen, keyboard, and mass storage device (and, we hoped, a printer) were to be built in so that the customer got a truly complete system, and so that we could control the appearance of characters and graphics."

Physically, the computer would be contained in an all-in-one case without cables. Raskin expected people to grow so attached to their Macs that they would never want to leave home without them (sound like any PowerBook users you know?), so portability was a key concern. He envisioned a weight under 20 pounds and an internal battery providing up to two hours of operation. His wish list also included an 8-bit microprocessor with 64 kilobytes (K) of random access memory (RAM), one serial port, modem, real-time clock, printer, 4- or 5-inch diagonal screen with bit-mapped graphics, and a 200K, 5.25-inch floppy disk drive all built in.

BASIC and FORTH programming languages were to be contained in read only memory (ROM), as were "self-instructional" programs that were so easy to use, manuals would be unnecessary. Raskin described a user interface in which everything—writing, calculating, drafting, painting, etc.—was accomplished in a graphical word processor-type environment with a few consistent and easily learned concepts. "For example, the calculator abilities will apply to numbers that are entered the same

way any text is entered. The traditional concept of an operating system is replaced by an extension of the idea of an on-line editor." While that may not sound much like the Mac as we know it today, his reasoning was that there should be no modes or levels, a concept that has endured.

Raskin even proposed an official name for his Macintosh computer: the Apple V. He figured that it could go into production by September 1981, for sale that Christmas with an initial end-user price of $500. As volume increased, he expected the price to drop to $300 after 18 months. Although Jobs strongly opposed the Macintosh when it was first proposed, Raskin nonetheless won the board's approval to begin a formal research project in September 1979.

"Jobs hated the idea. He ran around saying 'No! No! It'll never work.' He was one of the Macintosh's hardest critics and he was always putting it down at board meetings. When he became convinced that it would work, and that it would be an exciting new product, he started to take over...He was dead set against the Macintosh for the first two years. He said it was the dumbest thing on earth and that it would never sell. When he decided to take it over, he told everybody that he had invented it."

Jef Raskin
Accidental Millionaire,
p. 136-137

89

Careful What You Wish For

By September 27, 1979, a preliminary cost investigation revealed that with Apple's customary 400% cost of goods mark-up, there was no way Jef Raskin's proposed Macintosh could sell for the initial target price of $500, even without a disk drive and printer. A more realistic figure was $1,500 for a fully loaded Mac. On October 2, Steve Jobs told Raskin, "Don't worry about price, just specify the computer's abilities."

Raskin replied with a sarcastic memo specifying "a small, light-weight computer with an excellent, typewriter style keyboard. It is accompanied by a 96 character by 66 line display that has almost no depth, and a letter-quality printer that also doesn't weigh much, and takes ordinary paper and produces text at one page per second (not so fast so that you can't catch them as they come out). The printer can also produce any graphics the screen can show (with at least 1000 by 1200 points of res-olution). In color.

"The printer should weigh only a fraction of a pound, and never need a ribbon or mechanical adjustment. It should print in any font. There is about 200K bytes of main storage besides screen memory and a miniature, pocketable, storage element that holds a megabyte and costs $.50, in unit quantity.

"When you buy the computer, you get a free unlimited access to the ARPA net, the various timesharing services, and other informational, computer accessible data bases. Besides an unexcelled collection of application programs, the software includes BASIC, Pascal, LISP, FORTRAN, APL, PL\1, COBOL, and an emulator for every processor since the IBM 650.

"Let's include speech synthesis and recognition, with a vocab-ulary of 34,000 words. It can also synthesize music, even simu-late Caruso singing with the Mormon tabernacle choir, with variable reverberation.

> "Conclusion: starting with the abilities is nonsense. We must start both with a price goal, and a set of abilities, and keep an eye on today's and the immediate future's technology. These factors must be all juggled simultaneously."

Raskin was obviously kidding, and it's easy to see why his defiant manner rankled Jobs, but he unwittingly described many of the technologies which the Macintosh would come to possess in the decade following its introduction.

"With Steve [Jobs] you never know exactly where an idea comes from."

Steve Wozniak
Odyssey, pp. 140-141

As he brainstormed, Raskin kept coming up with more wonderful things to add to his computer (see "The Evolution of the Macintosh" later in this story). It didn't take him long to realize that he couldn't include everything he wanted and still produce a computer with a $500 price tag, so he settled on a new goal of $1,000. "There is no doubt that we want more—more mass storage, a built-in printer, color graphics—but we feel that low price and portability are the most important attributes, and we have kept strenuously to these goals," Raskin wrote in his memos.

Raskin needed someone to turn his ideas into prototypes. His former UCSD student, Bill Atkinson, was a respected member of the Lisa team, and he was impressed with the outstanding work Burrell Carver Smith was doing as a repairman in the Apple II maintenance department. Atkinson introduced Smith to Raskin as "the man who's going to design your Macintosh," to which Raskin replied, "We'll see about that." Smith whipped together a make-shift prototype using a Motorola 6809E microprocessor, a television monitor, and the guts of an Apple II. Duly impressed, Raskin made him the second member of the Mac team.

In time, Raskin took on an assistant, and Steve Wozniak began part-time work on the Mac, but Smith continued doing most of the detailed electronic

> **"The standard way [Jobs] operated was picking your brain. He would immediately poo-poo the idea, then a week later, he'd come back and say, 'Hey, I've got a great idea!' The idea that he gave back to you was your own. We called him the Reality Distortion Field."**
>
> **Jef Raskin**
>
> *Accidental Millionaire,* p. 138

design and breadboarding. This skeleton crew toiled in what had been Apple's first office and the birthplace of the Apple II and Lisa, Suite B-3 at 20833 Stevens Creek Boulevard, near the Good Earth restaurant in Cupertino. The Macintosh remained a research project and was not destined to become an actual product any time soon. Still, Raskin was obsessed with designing a computer that could be sold at a low price and manufactured in large quantities. Raskin did everything he could to "keep the project from burgeoning into a huge, expensive, and time-consuming effort."

Every feature required a trade-off between price and performance. They wanted a color monitor, but monochrome would have to do. The Lisa's 68000 microprocessor was desired, but the 6809E was much cheaper. A floppy disk drive would be great, but a digital cassette drive kept the cost down. More memory would nice, but 64K was considered adequate.

While Raskin's small team was quietly toiling in the Mac "skunkworks," turmoil was brewing elsewhere at Apple. Following the fateful visits to Xerox PARC, Jobs was making waves and enemies as he steered the Lisa project away from its original mandate as a $2,000 business computer into a much more expensive downsized Alto. In September 1980, the board of directors wanted to cancel the Macintosh project to concentrate on getting the jinxed Apple III out the door and getting the Lisa project under control, but Raskin pleaded for and won a three-month reprieve. During this time, president Michael M. Scott restructured the company and removed Jobs from the Lisa project. Jobs was furious, and to cool his heels Scott sent him out on the road to represent Apple prior to its initial public offering of stock on December 12, 1980.

With the IPO behind him, "Jobs was at loose ends because finally [the board] realized that he was totally incompetent as a manager," recalls Raskin. Jobs set his sights on the Macintosh project. As Andy Hertzfeld remembers it, "The Lisa team in general told Steve to fuck off. Steve said, 'I'll get this team that'll make a cheap computer and that will blow them off the face of the earth.' Then Steve saw that Raskin had critical mass: He had a hardware engineer and

> **"[Jobs] would try to push himself into everything. No matter what you were doing, he had to have something to do with it. Nobody at Apple wanted him involved with their projects. I had started the Macintosh team and we didn't want him either."**
>
> **Jef Raskin**
> *Accidental Millionaire*, p. 119

a software engineer. Since Steve was a bigger kid than Raskin, he said, 'I like that toy!' and took it." (*The Little Kingdom*, p. 130) Jobs tried renaming the computer "Bicycle" but nobody followed his lead, so he quietly dropped the idea.

The board was only too happy to let Jobs go off and spin his wheels on the Mac, which they viewed as a relatively unimportant research project. The board may have seen it that way, but Jobs viewed it as his opportunity to prove

Courtesy of Apple Computer, Inc.

Although Jobs' attempt to rename the Mac "Bicycle" failed, the concept survived as the logo for the Apple University Consortium's "Wheels for the Mind" promotion.

94

his worth as a technological innovator. At first Jobs was content to manage only the hardware side of the project, leaving Raskin in charge of software and documentation. "I was more interested in the interface than the chips inside," says Raskin, so the move didn't trouble him too much. Besides, with Jobs on board, perhaps the project would get the funding and support needed to actually create a product. Would it ever!

Raskin's Secret Memo

Steve Jobs began rubbing Jef Raskin the wrong way not long after muscling his way into the Mac project in January 1981. On February 19, 1981, a year before he resigned from Apple, Raskin sent a confidential, four-page memo to president Mike Scott detailing the specific problems he had working with Jobs. Here are the highlights:

1. Jobs regularly misses appointments.

2. He acts without thinking and with bad judgement.

3. He does not give credit where due.

4. Jobs often reacts ad hominem.

5. He makes absurd and wasteful decisions by trying to be paternal.

6. He interrupts and doesn't listen.

7. He does not keep promises or meet commitments.

8. He makes decisions ex cathedra.

9. Optimistic estimates.

10. Jobs is often irresponsible and inconsiderate.

11. He is a bad manager of software projects.

Soon after Jobs got involved, the Mac team took over the second floor in a small two-story building known as Texaco Towers due to its proximity to a gas station on the corner of De Anza and Stevens Creek Boulevards. (The gas station is vacant now, Texaco Towers is occupied by a different company, and Apple's City Center office complex across the street dominates the intersection.) There was no sign on 20431 Stevens Creek Boulevard, and the office wasn't even listed in the company's telephone directory. They were out in the boonies, which was perfect for the maverick project Jobs had in mind.

The Mac quickly went from being a research project to a full-blown product development effort with several dozen employees. Jobs seriously underestimated the amount of work yet to be done and the time it would take. He figured his team would ship the Macintosh in early 1982, just a year away. So confident was he in this prediction that he bet Lisa project manager John Couch $5,000 that the Mac would beat Lisa to market, even though the Lisa had been under serious development for more than two years and the Mac project was just now starting in earnest.

The Lisa appeared on January 19, 1983, more than a year before the Mac, and Steve Jobs actually paid off his $5,000 bet with John Couch.

One of the most significant advances in the Macintosh project had come when Smith figured out an ingenious way to replace the 6809E microprocessor with the more powerful 68000 used by the Lisa. Although Raskin resisted at first because it would drive up the cost of the computer, Jobs was all for the change. With Mac and Lisa sharing

the same microprocessor, it was easier for the Mac team
to use some of the Lisa technologies and software, including Atkinson's amazing QuickDraw routines. However,
Jobs steadfastly refused to make the Mac compatible with
the Lisa or vice versa.

> **"It's better to be a pirate than to join the Navy."**
>
> **Steve Jobs**, explaining the
> appeal of being part of the
> original Mac team
> *Odyssey*, p. 147

Symbolizing Jobs' defiant attitude and internecine rivalry
was the Jolly Roger that flew over the Mac team's newest
building, Bandley III (10460 Bandley Drive). Jobs referred
to his group as pirates, and in keeping with that spirit, he
began systematically raiding the Lisa project for key technologies and people (such as Atkinson and Steve Capps)
without regard for the overall well-being of Apple. As
Hertzfeld explained, "We looked for any place where we
could beg, borrow, or steal code."

Needless to say, the Mac began looking a lot like a little
Lisa. QuickDraw and other Lisa routines increased the
size of the Mac's ROM. It soon became apparent that the
Mac would share so such of the Lisa's interface that a
mouse was a necessity, much to Raskin's dismay; he was
leaning towards a lightpen or joystick as a graphic input
device. "I couldn't stand the mouse," says Raskin. "Jobs
gets 100 percent credit for insisting that a mouse be on
the Mac."

97

The Evolution of the Macintosh

Here's what the Mac specifications called for at various times during its development, based on official Apple documents.

DATE	5/29/79	9/27/79	9/28/79	10/12/79
Price	$500	$1,500	$500	$500

INTERNAL				
Processor	8-bit CPU	6809E	6809E	6809E
Memory	64K	64K	64K	64K
ROM	na	32K	32K	32K
Mass storage	200K 5.25" floppy	200K 5.25" floppy	optional	optional
Battery	2-hours	2-hours	2-hours	optional
Serial port	one	one	one	one
Modem	built-in	built-in	built-in	built-in
Real-Time clock	built-in	built-in	built-in	built-in

VIDEO				
Display	built-in	built-in	use TV	use TV
Diagonal	4" or 5"	4" or 5"	4" or 5"	4" or 5"
Characters	na	na	64 characters/line	64 characters/line
Pixels	na	na	na	na

INPUT				
Keyboard	built-in	built-in	built-in	built-in
Input device	na	na	na	na
Speech recognition	na	na	na	optional
Microphone	na	na	na	na

OUTPUT				
Printer	built-in	built-in	optional	optional
Speaker	na	na	na	built-in
Speech synthesis	na	na	na	optional

PHYSICAL				
Weight	20 pounds	na	10 pounds	na
Dimensions (WxD)	na	na	13" x 13" x 5"	na

SOFTWARE				
BASIC	built-in	built-in	built-in	na
Calculator	na	na	na	built-in
Communications	na	na	na	na
FORTH	built-in	na	na	na
Word processor	na	na	na	built-in

DATE	1/12/80	July-80	2/16/81	1/24/84
Price	$1,000	$1,300	$1,500	$2,495

INTERNAL

Processor	6809E	6809E	68000	68000
Memory	64K	64K	64K	128K
ROM	32K	32K	32K	64K
Mass storage	200K 5.25" floppy	200K cass drive	200K 5.25" floppy	400K 3.5" floppy
Battery	optional	optional	na	na
Serial port	one	one	one	two
Modem	built-in	built-in	built-in	na
Real-Time clock	built-in	built-in	built-in	built-in

VIDEO

Display	built-in	built-in	built-in	built-in
Diagonal	7 inches	7 inches	9 inches	9 inches
Characters	70 chars x 25 lines	72 chars x 25 lines	96 chars x 25 lines	na
Pixels	256 x 256	256 x 256	384 x 256	512 x 342

INPUT

Keyboard	built-in	built-in	built-in	detached
Input device	lightpen	joystick	joystick	mouse
Speech recognition	optional	optional	optional	na
Microphone	built-in	built-in	na	na

OUTPUT

Printer	optional	optional	optional	optional
Speaker	built-in	built-in	built-in	built-in
Speech synthesis	optional	optional	optional	limited

PHYSICAL

Weight	22 pounds	na	na	16.7 pounds
Dimensions (WxD)	na	na	na	13.5" x 9.7" x 10.9"

SOFTWARE

BASIC	disk resident	na	na	third-party
Calculator	built-in	built-in	built-in	desk accessory
Communications	na	built-in	built-in	na
FORTH	na	na	na	na
Word processor	built-in	built-in	built-in	MacWrite

Raskin did prevail in convincing Apple not to use a three-button mouse like the Alto, but rather, a one-button version that would be much easier for novices.

Working with Jerrold C. Manock, Jobs also pushed for the Mac's distinctive Cuisinart-inspired upright case design, and that necessitated a detached keyboard. With a rough idea of what the computer would look like physically, the design of the Mac's completely automated factory in Fremont, California got under way in the fall of 1981, even though Smith was still furiously working on yet another Mac prototype and many of the technical details had yet to be finalized. By February 1982, the case design was fixed and the signatures of all the team members were collected and transferred to the mold for the inside of the case (see the section entitled "Where Are They Now?").

Things were really picking up steam that February when Jobs approached Raskin and cavalierly announced "Well, I'm going to take over software and you can run documentation." That was more than Raskin could bear, and he replied, "No, you can have documentation too, I resign." The showdown was inevitable, according to Dan Kottke, one of the Mac engineers. "Jef Raskin and Steve Jobs both have large egos. Jef could have stayed on if he hadn't gone against Steve. But he feels very strongly about certain things and won't shut up."

Jobs and Markkula asked Raskin to reconsider, so he took a one-month leave of absence. Upon his return, Raskin was offered the leadership of a new research division. "Been there, done that," was the essence of Raskin's reply, so on March 1, 1982 he officially tendered his resignation.

Jobs was hell-bent on proving that he could produce a better computer than the Lisa, but it was becoming painfully apparent that the real competition was not the Lisa division, but rather, International Business Machines. IBM had introduced its Personal Computer on August 12, 1981 and the market had responded favorably, to say the least. Much to its dismay, Apple began losing market share (sliding from 29% to 24% in 1982) to what it considered a clearly inferior product.

Although the Mac team derided the IBM PC in public, privately they realized Big Blue was a formidable competitor and that they had better get their own product out the door. The window of opportunity was slowly closing, and if Apple didn't finish the Mac soon, it might lose out altogether. "We had been saying, 'We're going to finish in six months' for two years," recalls Hertzfeld, but Jobs laid down the law and pushed to ship Macintosh on May 16, 1983 at the National Computer Conference in Anaheim, California.

Courtesy of Peter Stember and Apple Computer, Inc.

Chris Espinosa

101

"When we started this project, IBM didn't have a machine. But we looked very carefully at their PC when they released it. At first it was embarrassing how bad their machine was. Then we were horrified [at its success]. We hope the Macintosh will show people what the IBM PC was—a half-assed, hackneyed attempt at the old technology."

Chris Espinosa, Mac documentation leader

Rolling Stone, March 1, 1984, p. 41

Facing a hard deadline forced the team to make several major decisions which resulted in a sort of domino effect. High-resolution graphics had always been a primary goal for the Mac, but even as late as 1982 the 9-inch diagonal monitor could display only 384 by 256 pixels. That was certainly acceptable for graphics, but not exactly at the leading edge of technology. George Crow, analog manager, increased the resolution to the final dimensions of 512 by 342 pixels, allowing the Mac to display 80 columns of fixed-pitch (monospaced) text, considered essential for acceptance in the business market.

With the increased resolution of the bit-mapped display, more memory was needed. Like Raskin before him, Jobs thought that 64 kilobytes of memory was acceptable, but the team convinced him that 128 kilobytes was needed (actually, they wanted more, so they secretly designed a way to easily increase memory by swapping chips).

More memory meant larger programs, and the 200K, 5.25-inch floppy disk drive no longer seemed like an adequate mass-storage device. Unbeknownst to Jobs, his engineers had anticipated this problem and were already working on a solution based upon a new 400K, 3.5-inch drive from Sony.

The May 1983 ship date came and went and still the Mac wasn't complete. Each of the hardware changes took longer than expected, but nothing took as much time as completing the software. Even though Jobs had assembled many of Apple's brightest minds in the Mac division, doing the impossible takes time, especially when you have a perfectionist like Jobs as a boss. "Tact is a word you don't use to describe him," says Espinosa. "Steve will just walk up to your desk, look

"We decided to go with the Sony disks because they were able to almost double our capacity. They're also much easier to handle than the fragile 5.25-inch floppies."

Barbara Koalkin,
Macintosh product
marketing manager

Computers & Electronics,
March 1984, p. 48

at what you're doing and say, 'That's shit.'" (*Rolling Stone*, March 1, 1984, p. 41)

Macintosh Timeline

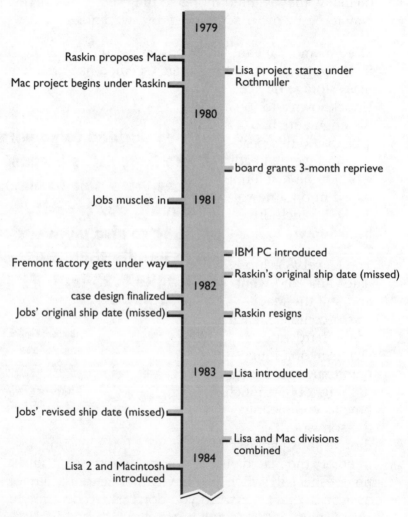

	1979
Raskin proposes Mac	
Mac project begins under Raskin	Lisa project starts under Rothmuller
	1980
	board grants 3-month reprieve
Jobs muscles in	1981
	IBM PC introduced
Fremont factory gets under way	Raskin's original ship date (missed)
case design finalized	1982
Jobs' original ship date (missed)	Raskin resigns
	1983 Lisa introduced
Jobs' revised ship date (missed)	
	Lisa and Mac divisions combined
Lisa 2 and Macintosh introduced	1984

Despite the unbelievable pressure they were under, Mac team members were spotted around the Apple campus wearing T-shirts that read "Working 80 hours a week and loving it," and some had even crossed out the "80" and replaced it with "90." This dedicated band of pirates had bought into Jobs' dream of changing the world, and they worked themselves to exhaustion to make the Macintosh the best damn computer they could.

> "He's a very motivational kind of guy, like a Roman legion commander. He really knows how to motivate small groups of people to produce."
>
> **Joanna Hoffman**, describing Jobs' managerial style
> *Computers & Electronics*, March 1984, p. 49

"He would have made an excellent King of France."

Jef Raskin

Time, January 3, 1983, p. 26

Finally, after spending $78 million in development costs, Apple introduced the Macintosh to wildly cheering crowds at the annual stockholders' meeting on January 24, 1984 (ironically, the stock closed down 1 5/8 at $27.25). The Macintosh was considerably smaller, faster, and cheaper than the ground-breaking Lisa introduced the previous year. It had a 68000 microprocessor running at 7.83 MHz, 128K of RAM, one 400K, 3.5-inch floppy disk drive, and a 9-inch monochrome display. The Mac came bundled with MacPaint (written by Bill Atkinson), MacWrite (written by Randy Wigginton), and the Finder (written by Bruce Horn and Steve Capps).

Courtesy of Apple Computer, Inc.

Some major players in the Macintosh team were (left to right) Bill Atkinson, Andy Hertzfeld, Chris Espinosa, George Crow, Joanna Hoffman, Burrell Smith, and Jerry Manock.

> **"The next generation of interesting software will be done on the Macintosh, not the IBM PC."**
>
> **Bill Gates,**
> Microsoft
> chairman
> *BusinessWeek*,
> November 26,
> 1984, p. 154

Software Seed List

Apple was astute enough to realize that in breaking with the IBM-DOS standard, the Mac must have a wide variety of third-party products available as soon after introduction as possible. Evangelists (yup, that's what it said on their business cards) Mike Boich and Guy Kawasaki approached a wide variety of software publishers and hardware manufacturers and begged, bribed, and berated them until they promised to create products for the Mac, even though that entailed the purchase of a Lisa as a development system.

By the time the Macintosh Product Introduction Plan was codified on October 7, 1983, the following developers had been selected "according to their marketing ability, technical expertise, end-user support capabilities, and desirability of application." Just for kicks, tally up the number of early Mac developers that are still around today.

Aardvark	DB Master Associates
Accountant's Microsystem	Debbie Wilrett
Addison-Wesley	Desktop Computer Software
Applied Software Technology	Digital Marketing
Ashton-Tate	Digital Research
Ask Micro	Dilithium Software
BBN Communications Corp.	Dow Jones
Bill Duvall	Execuware
Brøderbund	Fox and GellerGreat Plains
BPI	Harper and Row
Brady Company	Harris Labs
Business Solutions	Harvard Software
CBS	Hayden Software
Chang Labs	Howard Software Services
Compu-Law	Infocom
CompuServe	John Wiley and Sons
Continental Software	Kriya Systems
Cygnet Technologies	LCSI
Data Resources	Lightning Software
Datasoft	Living Videotext
Davong Systems Inc.	Lotus Development Corp.

McGraw-Hill	Sir Tech
Mead	Sirius
MECC	Software Arts
Microcom	Software Publishing Corp.
Microsoft	Software Technology for
Northwest Instruments	Computers
Orchid Systems	Sorcim
Peachtree/MSA	State of the Art
Peat-Marwick	Synapse
Persyst	T/Maker Company
Phone 1, Inc.	Tecmar
Plato	The Source
Quark	Tom Snyder Productions
Random House	Trade Plus
Reston Publishing Co.	Tronix
Richard D. Irwin	TSC
Scientific Marketing Inc.	University of Waterloo
Sierra On-Line	Volition Systems
Simon and Schuster	Winterhalter, Inc.

"Good software is like pornography: very difficult to describe but you know it when you see it. Good software is art: you can see the 'soul' of a programmer or programmers. Good software is fun: it should bring a smile to your face when you use it. Good software causes an erection in the mind of a software evangelist."

Guy Kawasaki
The Macintosh Reader,
pp. 183-184

Courtesy of Guy Kawasaki

Guy Kawasaki

Up until the very last moment before introduction, Apple executives argued over the Mac's price. Jobs had hoped that the Mac could sell for $1,495. As it turned out, the Mac cost $500 to build (83% materials, 16% overhead, 1% labor), and with Apple's standard mark-up, the price should have been $1,995. But president John Sculley had ordered an aggressive $15-million, 100-day advertising blitz which kicked off with the *1984* commercial during Super Bowl XVIII. To pay for this campaign, Sculley tacked on a hefty premium and the list price for the original Mac was set at $2,495. So much for Raskin's $500 computer which would appeal to the person in the street. The Macintosh was now "The Computer for the Rest of Us," defined as anyone with several grand burning a hole in their pockets.

The Great Mac Giveaway

In an effort to curry favor with celebrities and generate some favorable press upon the introduction of the Macintosh, Apple gave 50 machines to a select group of luminaries and key decision makers. Among them:

Bob Ciano, *Life* magazine art director

Dianne Feinstein, San Francisco mayor

Milton Glaser, designer

Jim Henson, Muppet creator

Lee Iacocca, Chrysler chairman

Sean Lennon, son of late Beatle, John Lennon

Maya Lin, Vietnam Veterans Memorial designer

Peter Martins, ballet master

David Rockefeller, really rich guy

Stephen Sondheim, composer and lyricist

Ted Turner, entrepreneur

Kurt Vonnegut, novelist

Andy Warhol, pop artist

"**The Mac is meant to supplant the PC on the desks of corporate America, just as the PC supplanted our own Apples over the last 18 months.**"

John Sculley

Forbes, February 13, 1984, p. 39

Even at its artificially inflated price, Jobs predicted Apple would sell 50,000 Macs in the 100 days following introduction and half a million units by the end of 1984; Sculley's figure was a more realistic 250,000 units. Although they were both way off base with their annual forecasts, Apple reached the 100-day goal on Day 73 (April 6), and managed to sell 72,000 Macs by Day 100 (May 3). Koalkin claimed "We could have sold 200,000 Macintoshes if we could have built them." (*USA Today*, May 3, 1984)

Confident that sales would pick up during the Christmas months, Apple began building inventory at a rate of 110,000 units a month. Unfortunately, after the initial burst of sales to early adopters (plus computer dealers, developers, and college students who paid far less than list price thanks to special promotions), Mac sales tapered off dramatically to roughly 20,000 Macs a month. In fact, it took until September 1985 to sell 500,000 Macs, until March 1987 to reach the one million mark, and until February 1993 to surpass the 10 million milestone.

On March 17, 1987, Apple pulled six Mac Plus computers off the assembly line and designated each the one millionth Mac. In recognition of his being the true father of the Macintosh, Jef Raskin was presented with one of these Macs. Ironically, this Mac Plus was the first Macintosh Raskin ever owned. It's still in use today at his home in Pacifica, California, along with a PowerBook 180.

Canon Cat

In 1987, Jef Raskin finally got his chance to more fully realize the embodiment of his original Macintosh design goals with a "work processor" called the Canon Cat, which had word processor, spreadsheet, and telecommunications features built in. Most people have never heard of the Cat, and with good reason. After only six months on the market, Canon abruptly dropped the Cat without explanation. It's not as if the Canon Cat was a dog, if you'll forgive the pun. The $1,495 Cat was well received by the public, selling a respectable 20,000 units and winning many design awards. Why, then, did Canon put the Cat to sleep?

Over the years, Raskin received two anonymous telephone calls from people claiming to be Canon employees. They offered conflicting motives for Canon's actions. One explained

Courtesy of Jef Raskin

The Canon Cat looks suspiciously like Raskin's early Mac prototypes.

that the electronic typewriter division and the computer division were fighting for control of the Cat. The new president of Canon USA wanted to exert his power and told the two divisions to settle the matter quickly or he would do it for them. They continued to fight over the Cat, so he killed the project outright to teach them a lesson.

The second caller painted a more sinister scenario involving Raskin's old nemesis, Steve Jobs. Shortly after the Cat was introduced, Canon was exploring the possibility of investing in Jobs' new venture, NeXT. Unwilling to share the corporate attention of Canon with Raskin, Jobs told Canon that unless they dropped the Cat, he wouldn't allow them to invest in NeXT. Although Raskin has never been able to verify either story, Canon did pay $100 million for a 16.67% share of NeXT in June 1989. Kinda makes you wonder...

1984: The Greatest Commercial That Almost Never Aired

Every true Macintosh fanatic has seen, or at least heard about, the famous *1984* television commercial that heralded the introduction of the Macintosh. The spot, with its distinctive cinéma vérité Orwellian vision, is indelibly imprinted in the minds of Mac users the world over. Now, for the first time, the whole truth can be told. What you don't know about the commercial will surprise you, what you think you know is probably wrong.

> **"Am I getting anything I should give a shit about?"**
>
> **Steve Jobs**, upon first meeting Lee Clow
> *West of Eden*, p. 87

First of all, the commercial was not inspired by the Mac. In late 1982, Apple's advertising agency, Chiat/Day, had devised a corporate print campaign for *The Wall Street Journal* featuring the Apple II that was designed to play off George Orwell's totalitarian vision of the future.

"Six months before we knew about Mac, we had this new ad that read, 'Why 1984 won't be like *1984*.'" reveals Lee Clow, creative director at Chiat/Day. "It explained Apple's philosophy and purpose—that people, not just government and big corporations, should run technology. If computers aren't to take over our lives, they have to be accessible."

On January 24th, Apple Computer will introduce Macintosh. And you'll see why 1984 won't be like "1984."

Courtesy of Apple Computer, Inc.

This famous tag line wasn't inspired by the Mac.

The ad never ran and was filed away, only to be dusted off in the spring of 1983 by Steve Hayden, the agency's copywriter, and Brent Thomas, the art director, who were looking for some hook to make a bold statement about the incredible new Macintosh. With considerable reworking, the Chiat/Day team put together a storyboard of the *1984* commercial they proposed to shoot.

The mini-movie would show an athletic young woman, chased by helmeted storm troopers, burst into a dank auditorium in which row upon row of slack-jawed, drone-like workers watched an image of Big Brother spouting an ideological diatribe on a huge screen. The heroine, wearing bright red jogging shorts and a white Macintosh tee-shirt, would smash the screen with a base-ball bat (later changed to a sledgehammer for dramatic effect) and a refreshing burst of fresh air would pass over the masses as they literally "saw the light."

In the closing shot, a solemn voice would intone, "On January 24th, Apple Computer will introduce Macintosh. And you'll see why 1984 won't be like *1984*."

After Chiat/Day presented the storyboard to Apple, John Sculley was apprehensive, but Steve Jobs insisted that the Mac deserved such a radical spot. They gave the authorization to shoot the commercial and purchase time to air it during the upcoming Super Bowl.

Courtesy of Apple Computer, Inc.

The beautiful, athletic heroine was the embodiment of Apple's youthful self-image.

The Making of a Legend

On the strength of his successful science-fiction films *Alien* and *Blade Runner*, Chiat/Day gave Ridley Scott a budget of $900,000 to direct the *1984* spot as well as a Lisa commercial called *Alone Again*, in which, believe it or not, Apple actually emphasized the fact that the Lisa was incompatible with all established standards.

In September, Scott assembled a cast of 200 for a week of filming at London's Shepperton Studios. To play the part of the despondent, bald-headed workers, Scott recruited authentic British skinheads and paid amateurs $125 a day to shave off their hair. Casting the heroine proved trickier.

Many of the professional fashion models and actresses had difficulty spinning in place and then accurately throwing the sledgehammer as called for in the script. In fact, one errant toss almost killed an old lady walking down a path in Hyde Park where the casting call was being held. As luck would have it, one model, Anya Major, was also an experienced discus thrower and was hired to play the female lead because she looked the part and didn't get dizzy when spinning around preparing to hurl the hammer.

When the rough cut was assembled, Chiat/Day proudly presented it to Jobs and Sculley. Jobs loved the commercial and Sculley thought it was crazy enough that it just might work. In October, the commercial was aired publicly for the first time at Apple's annual sales conference in Honolulu's civic auditorium. The 750 sales reps went wild when they saw the piece.

Jobs and Sculley clearly thought they had a winner on their hands, so in late December, they asked marketing manager Mike Murray to screen the commercial for the other members of Apple's board of directors: A. C. "Mike" Markkula Jr. (Apple founder), Dr. Henry E. Singleton (Teledyne founder), Arthur Rock (venture capitalist), Peter O. Crisp (managing partner in Rockefeller's Venrock Associates), and Philip S. Schlein (CEO of Macy's California).

When the lights came back up after the spot played, the room on De Anza Boulevard was silent. Schlein was sitting with his head on the table. Markkula stared in amazement. Murray thought Markkula was overcome by the wonderful commercial until he broke the silence to ask, "Who wants to move to find a new agency?" Sculley recalls, "The others just looked at each other, dazed expressions on their faces...Most of them felt it was the worst commercial they had ever seen. Not a single outside board member liked it." (*Odyssey*, pp. 176-177)

"Some of them liked it, some of them didn't."

Steve Jobs, spin doctor, describing the board's reaction to *1984*.

San Jose Mercury News, January 24, 1984, p. 7E

The board hadn't demanded the commercial be killed, nonetheless Sculley asked Chiat/Day to sell back the one and one half minutes of Super Bowl television time that they had purchased. The original plan was to play the full-length, 60-second *1984* spot to catch everyone's attention, then hammer home the message during a subsequent commercial break with an additional airing of an edited 30-second version.

Defying Sculley's request, Jay Chiat told his media diretor, Camille Johnson, "Just sell off the thirty." Johnson laughed, thinking it would be impossible to sell any of the time at so late a date, but miraculously, she managed to find a buyer for the 30-second slot. That still left Apple with a 60-second slot for which it had paid $800,000.

Perhaps seeking to cover himself in the event the commercial flopped, Sculley left the decision of whether to run *1984* up to Bill Campbell (VP of marketing) and E. Floyd Kvamme (executive VP of marketing and sales). If they couldn't sell the Super Bowl minute and decided against airing *1984*, the backup plan was to run *Manuals*, a rather straightforward product-benefit spot that challenged viewers to decide which was the more sophisticated computer: the IBM PC, with its huge pile of documentation that came crashing down beside the computer, or the Macintosh, with its light-as-a-feather user's guide floating to rest next to the mouse.

Woz's Wonderful Reaction

Still pushing for *1984*, Jobs sought the support of Steve Wozniak, who normally didn't like to get involved in such political issues. Recalls Wozniak, "One evening I was over at the Macintosh group, which I was about to join, and Steve grabbed me and said 'Hey, come over here and look at this.' He pulled up a 3/4-inch VCR and played the ad. I was astounded. I thought it was the most incredible thing.

"Then he told me that the board decided not to show it. He didn't say why. I was so shocked. Steve said we were going to run it during the Super Bowl. I asked how much it was going to cost, and he told me $800,000. I said, 'Well, I'll pay half of it if you will.' I figured it was a problem with the company justifying the expenditure. I thought an ad that was so great a piece of science fiction should have its chance to be seen."

> **"We were so convinced we had a major product statement that we weren't worried about the product living up to the commercial."**
>
> **E. Floyd Kvamme**
>
> *1984 Revisited* by Verne Gay,
> *Madison Avenue*

Campbell and Kvamme threw caution to the wind and decided to run the *1984* commercial after all, kicking off a $15-million, 100-day advertising blitz for the Mac. Fortunately for Wozniak, Jobs didn't take him up on his offer to pony up half the cost. On January 22, 1984, the controversial commercial aired to an audience of 96

120

million early in the third quarter of Super Bowl XVIII, in which the Los Angeles Raiders defeated the Washington Redskins 38 to 9 in Tampa Stadium.

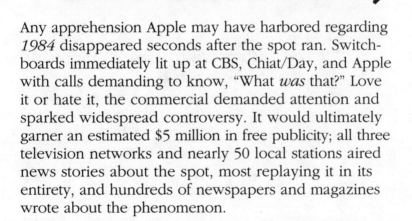

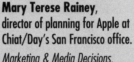

"We wanted people to say, 'What the hell is this product?' The idea was to use the commercial as a tease, not a product introduction; to make sure the world knew a new product was here and that it was a significant event."

Mary Terese Rainey,
director of planning for Apple at Chiat/Day's San Francisco office.
Marketing & Media Decisions,
November 1984, p. 55

Any apprehension Apple may have harbored regarding *1984* disappeared seconds after the spot ran. Switchboards immediately lit up at CBS, Chiat/Day, and Apple with calls demanding to know, "What *was* that?" Love it or hate it, the commercial demanded attention and sparked widespread controversy. It would ultimately garner an estimated $5 million in free publicity; all three television networks and nearly 50 local stations aired news stories about the spot, most replaying it in its entirety, and hundreds of newspapers and magazines wrote about the phenomenon.

> "It broke all the rules; and the reaction has been, in a word, unprecedented."
>
> **Steve Hayden**
> *San Francisco Chronicle*,
> February 17, 1984, p. 31

A.C. Nielson estimated the commercial reached 46.4 percent of the households in America, a full 50 percent of the nation's men, and 36 percent of the women. The commercial recorded astronomical recall scores and went on to win the Grand Prize of Cannes as well as over 30 other advertising industry awards.

> "It was all this horseshit from people who didn't have the balls to produce something like *1984*."
>
> **Lee Clow**, dismissing his competitors' negative reactions to the commercial.
> *Madison Avenue*

The *1984* commercial was the first example of what Sculley called "event marketing," the goal of which is to create a promotion so ground-breaking that it deserves as much coverage as the product itself. Apple fed the media frenzy surrounding *1984* by announcing that the commercial would never be aired again.

To this day, if you ask most Apple employees about the commercial, they will proudly claim that the only time Apple ever paid to run the commercial was during the Super Bowl. It's been repeated convincingly so many times by so many sincere people that it's now accepted as gospel. Hate to break it to you, but it's a lie.

In keeping with industry tradition, Chiat/Day paid $10 to run *1984* in the 1:00 A.M. sign-off slot on December 15, 1983 at a small television station (KMVT, Channel 11) in Twin Falls, Idaho, thereby ensuring that the commercial would qualify for that year's advertising awards. And beginning on January 17, the 30-second version of the commercial appeared in ScreenVision, an advertising medium played in movie theaters before previews and feature presentations (some theater owners loved the commercial so much that they continued running it for months without pay).

At the same time, a five-day teaser campaign began running a full schedule during prime time in America's ten largest television markets (encompassing 30 percent of the nation's viewers), plus the relatively unimportant television market of West Palm Beach, Florida, right next door to IBM's PC headquarters.

> **"I would love to know what they're saying in Boca Raton," mused Jobs the day after the Super Bowl.**

Ironically, it was during the same game that IBM launched the ad campaign for its ill-fated, low-cost PCjr computer which had just begun shipping to dealers. The light-hearted commercial depicted Charlie Chaplin wheeling the PCjr into a room in a baby carriage as the announcer introduced "the bright little addition to the family." Jobs would later remark, "I expected the computer to wet all over the television set." Reflecting on IBM's use of Charlie Chaplin's Modern Times character, Jean-Louis Gassée found it "surprising that the Little Tramp, symbolizing the worst aspects of the assembly line, was chosen to advertise a company that is a humanistic one in every other way." (*The Third Apple*, p. 56)

"Luck is a force of nature. Everything seemed to conspire to make *1984* a hit: the timing, the product, the industry. Using the *1984* theme was such an obvious idea that I was worried someone else would beat us to it, but nobody did."

Steve Hayden, explaining
the success of *1984*

Apple spent more than $2.5 million to buy all 40 pages of advertising in a special 1984 election issue of *Newsweek* magazine. At the time, John Sculley remarked, "It's unclear whether Apple has an advertising insert in *Newsweek* or whether *Newsweek* has an insert in an Apple brochure." (*San Francisco Chronicle*, November 8, 1984, p. 31)

Big Brother Speaks

As *1984* was originally conceived, Big Brother did not have a speaking role, but director Ridley Scott wanted to give him some lines. Copywriter Steve Hayden objected at first, but agreed to put something together when Scott threatened to write the lines himself. Apple vehemently denied that the propaganda-spouting Big Brother character in its *1984* commercial represented its $40-billion competitor, IBM.

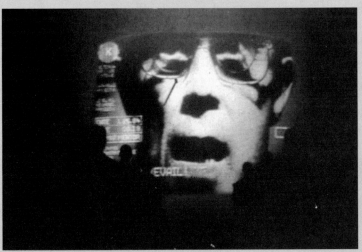

Courtesy of Apple Computer, Inc.

Is Big Blue Big Brother?

Decide for yourself as you read Big Brother's harangue from the full-length, 60-second commercial:

"My friends, each of you is a single cell in the great body of the State. And today, that great body has purged itself of parasites. We have triumphed over the unprincipled dissemination of facts. The thugs and wreckers have been cast out. And the poisonous weeds of disinformation have been consigned to the dustbin of history. Let each and every cell rejoice! For today we celebrate the first, glorious anniversary of the Information Purification Directive! We have created, for the first time in all history, a garden of pure ideology, where each worker may bloom secure from the pests of contradictory and confusing truths. Our Unification of Thought is a more powerful weapon than any fleet or army on Earth! We are one people. With one will. One resolve. One cause. Our enemies shall talk themselves to death. And we will bury them with their own confusion!"

The Mac
Meets the Press

When the Macintosh was introduced in 1984, Apple's public relations and marketing departments performed miracles, managing to secure more coverage for its newborn than any other computer in history. Looking back with the aid of 20/20 hindsight, read the following excerpts from several of the major computer publications of the time and decide for yourself which journalists were on the mark when it came to assessing the original Macintosh.

Byte

"The Lisa computer was important because it was the first commercial product to use the mouse-window-desktop environment. The Macintosh is equally important because it makes that same environment very affordable.

"The Macintosh will have three important effects. First, like the Lisa, it will be imitated but not copied...Those companies that try to imitate the Mac on other machines will have trouble matching its price/performance combination.

"Second, the Macintosh will secure the place of the Sony 3.5-inch disk as the magnetic medium of choice for the next generation of personal computers.

127

"Third, the Macintosh will increase Apple's reputation in the market...Many business users will stay with the 'safer' IBM PC. However, people new to computing and those who are maverick enough to see the value and promise of the Mac will favor it. The Mac will delay IBM's domination of the personal computer market.

"Overall, the Macintosh is a very important machine that, in my opinion, replaces the Lisa as the most important development in computers in the last five years. The Macintosh brings us one step closer to the ideal of computer as appliance. We're not there yet—at least, not until the next set of improvements (which, in this industry, we may see fairly soon). Who knows who the next innovator will be?" (Gregg Williams, February 1984)

Computer & Electronics

"Despite [the omissions of color and a parallel port], Macintosh is an impressive product and worthy of taking the 'less-traveled' road. Apparently, much of Apple's future depends on Macintosh, so its success or failure will truly make 'all the difference.'" (Vanessa Schnatmeier, March 1984, p. 48)

Creative Computing

"In its current form, the Macintosh is the distilled embodiment of a promise: that software can be intuitively easy to use, while remaining just as powerful as anything else around...It should be obvious to you now that the Mac does represent a significant break-though, both in hardware and in software. It should also be clear that the true

concern is whether the machine will live up to its unde-
niable promise. Fine. It is now time to lay out the 'bads.'

- The Macintosh does not have enough
  RAM memory.
- Single microfloppy storage is slow
  and inadequate.
- There are no internal expansion slots
  or external expansion busses.
- MacWrite has some severe limitations.
- The system is monochrome only.
- MS-DOS compatibility is ruled out.
- The Macintosh will not multitask.
- You can't use a Mac away from a desk.
- MacPaint has an easel size limitation.
- Forget about external video.
- Macintosh software development
  is an involved process.

"I simply wonder if this standard can be upheld. The
thought first occurred to me as I played around with
Microsoft BASIC. A BASIC program running on the Mac
looks very much like a BASIC program running on any
other machine, except for its windows. Without the icon/
window/menu shells, the Mac is reduced to a rather average machine.

"It is up to talented programmers to make the most of
Macintosh ROM in every program they develop. With it
they can meet the ambitious promise that is the Apple
Macintosh. Otherwise the Mac may never develop the
staying power it needs.

129

"We are still quite some distance from the ideal machine Alan Kay envisioned back in 1971 and christened the 'Dynabook.' This is a computer the size of a [Tandy] Model 100 with the power of a hundred Macs. In a recent interview, he rather cynically predicted that it would be the Japanese who would make the Dynabook a reality. He told Allen Muro of *St. Mac* magazine that the Macintosh was in point of fact 'no big deal.'

"That's the problem with people who are vastly ahead of their time. The times never seem to catch up. The Mac clocks in at 8 MHz, but Kay is already imagining what he could do with 12 MHz. In my last vestiges of prideful nationalism, I only hope it is Apple, not NEC, that introduces a 1000K 12 MHz machine two years from now. Perhaps I will write about it using a truly professional word processor running on a 512K hard disk Macintosh. Of course Kay will still be cranky with it, even when it does happen. If only he had 20 MHz and 5000K in a case the size of a box of Milk Duds. Then he could really make things happen. Well if anybody can pull off that kind of miracle, it is probably Apple. Those folks show a lot of promise." (John J. Anderson, July 1984)

inCider

"The Macintosh is the best hardware value in the history (short though it may be) of the personal computer industry. It is a machine which will appeal to the masses of people who have neither the time nor the inclination to embark upon the long learning process required to master the intricacies of the present generation of personal computers. Barring unforeseen technical glitches and assuming that a reasonable software library is in place by the end of the year, the Macintosh should establish itself as the next standard in personal computers." (Bob Ryan, March 1984, p. 47)

InfoWorld

"Considering all of the hoopla that has preceded the Mac's introduction, we are still greatly impressed with Apple's new product. The Macintosh is a well-designed personal computer that, dollar for dollar, represents the most advanced personal computer to date. The MC68000 processor, the 3.5-inch variable-speed disk drive, the high-resolution display, the advanced operating system and user interface as well as the rich use of graphics make this machine superior to the rest of the pack. In our opinion, the success of the Macintosh will be determined by Apple's ability to provide or to encourage others to supply hardware expansions and exciting and usable software. We think Apple has at least one thing right—the Macintosh is the one machine with the potential to challenge IBM's hold on the market." (Thomas Neudecker, March 26, 1984, p. 90)

Microcomputing

"Macintosh is a machine that is fun. As an Apple II owner, I felt uncomfortable and even suspicious about a computer that is so easy to operate. Missing was the familiar Applesoft prompt—a PR#6 before reading a disk. What I found was a machine that was so easy to operate that my eight-year-old would constantly pester me to use the Macintosh while I was writing this review. Within an hour she was well-versed in the terminology and in how to use the machine. This type of ease of use may create some resentment in the hacker in you—the machine consciously places distance between you and the operating system. In the Macintosh case, the term user transparent would be more accurate [than] user friendly. Macintosh represents state-of-the-art windowing technology at a price you might pay for just window software for the IBM PC. Its speed and sophistication place it above any window products I've seen for the PC. Its size [makes] it a welcome appliance on a desk. Plans for integrating Macintosh into a networked office system containing a Lisa at its heart and Macintoshes on most desks will appeal to almost anyone who, in Apple terminology, is a 'knowledge worker.' Whether or not you're in the market for a computer, experience a Macintosh. I bet that you will want one!" (Keith Thompson, March 1984, p. 72)

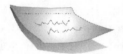

Formula for determining when a Macintosh was manufactured: The first letter of the serial number represents the location of the factory, the next digit is the year of manufacture, and the following two digits are the week. For example, if the serial number is F744641M5010, then the computer would have been manufactured in Fremont, California during the 44th week of 1987.

"**Borland founder Philippe Kahn was half right in Janurary 1985, when he called the early Macintosh 'a piece of shit.' It was underpowered, had very little software, no hard drive, no compelling application like desktop publishing, and it was marketed by a company that seemed to be near death. I can't help but be amused by all the pumped-up bravado I hear and read about the people who created the Macintosh. To hold up the Macintosh experience as an example of how to create a great product, launch an industry, or spark a revolution, is a cruel joke. Anyone who models their business startup on the Macintosh startup is doomed to failure. Miracles, like the Macintosh, can only happen once.**"

David Bunnell, originial
publisher of *Macworld*
The Macintosh Reader, p. 43

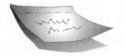

Q. How many Macintosh Division employees do you need to change a light bulb?

A. One. He holds the light bulb up and lets the universe revolve around him.

The Seybold Report on Professional Computing

"It's entirely reasonable to expect Mac itself to grow over time. The first logical step would be to give Mac an external Winchester [hard disk drive] like that used on Lisa...Other future steps will almost certainly include higher-capacity drives...We would certainly expect that Apple will eventually be able to offer 800K double-sided drives. Along with progress in disks, we can expect progress in computer memories...Replacing the current 64K memory chips with the new 256K chips expected onto the market this year could increase the RAM memory from 128K to 512K without requiring a larger circuit board. The machine we would dearly love to have when it becomes available would be a Macintosh with 512K of RAM, an external Winchester disk, and an 800K internal disk.

"On the positive side, everyone in our organization who has used the Mac, and every family member we have pressed into service to help us with this evaluation, has been enthusiastic about the design of the machine and the user interface. The longer you use it, the more you realize how good it is...Apple got a lot of things right with Macintosh. In many ways Mac represents the direction that desktop computers are (or at least should be) going:

- The computer as an appliance. No electronic skills required.

- A system which is truly easy to use. It is a pleasure for everyone from the computerphobe to the computer-jock.

- A compact, transportable package.

134

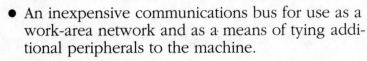

- A beautiful screen display and very quick graphics.

- An inexpensive communications bus for use as a work-area network and as a means of tying additional peripherals to the machine.

- Attractive pricing.

- A great deal of personality and user appeal.

"Apple also got some important things wrong. Our biggest worry is that Mac may be under-configured...But the dumbest thing Apple did with the whole development effort was to allow two different operating environments for Mac and Lisa." (Jonathan and Andrew M. Seybold, Vol. 2, No. 6, PC-25 through PC-27)

Bold Intros and Quiet Exits

The prices listed in the following timeline are for the least-expensive Macintosh models available. Keep in mind that some models come complete with monitors, keyboard, and mouse, whereas these are optional on other models.

"The Mac is the first computer good enough to be criticized."

Alan Kay, Apple Fellow
InfoWorld, June 11, 1984,
p. 59

Beginning in October 1993, Apple replaced its suggested retail prices (SRP) with what it calls ApplePrices, which are much closer to the actual street price customers find in stores. Apple does not release any pricing information for its Performa models, preferring to let the retailers establish whatever prices they wish.

On average, just before a model is discontinued, it's selling for 22 percent less than its price at introduction. In many cases, the model has had features (such as more memory, a larger hard drive, etc.) added to it over time, so it's a much better buy than the percentage decline indicates at first glance.

Can this Bird Fly?

Apple's top-of-the-line, 68040-based PowerBook 540/540c project was code-named Blackbird, after the Stealth fighter because both feature dark colors, curves, and speed. However, it's known informally inside Apple as the Spruce Goose because some people feel that introducing a 7-pound laptop in 1994 is as ill-fated an idea as Howard Hughes' huge air- craft which flew only once. On a related note, the Blackbird's innovative new Trackpad was code-named Midas, after the Phrygian king who had the power of turning whatever he touched into gold.

Intro and Exit Timeline

Introduced (Intro Price)　　　　　Discontinued (Exit Price)

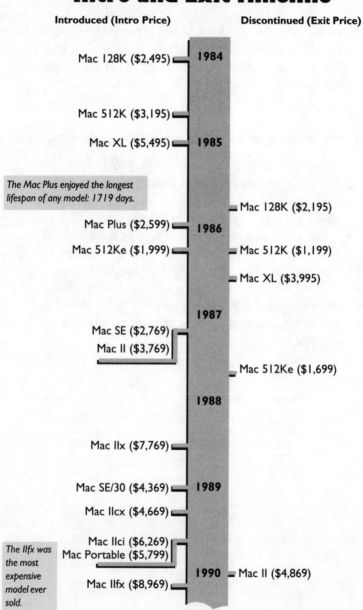

Mac 128K ($2,495) — **1984**

Mac 512K ($3,195) —

Mac XL ($5,495) — **1985**

*The Mac Plus enjoyed the longest
lifespan of any model: 1719 days.*

— Mac 128K ($2,195)

Mac Plus ($2,599) — **1986**

Mac 512Ke ($1,999) — — Mac 512K ($1,199)

— Mac XL ($3,995)

1987

Mac SE ($2,769) —

Mac II ($3,769)

— Mac 512Ke ($1,699)

1988

Mac IIx ($7,769) —

Mac SE/30 ($4,369) — **1989**

Mac IIcx ($4,669) —

Mac IIci ($6,269)
Mac Portable ($5,799)

*The IIfx was
the most
expensive
model ever
sold.*

1990 — Mac II ($4,869)

Mac IIfx ($8,969) —

138

Intro and Exit Timeline

Introduced (Intro Price)   **Discontinued (Exit Price)**

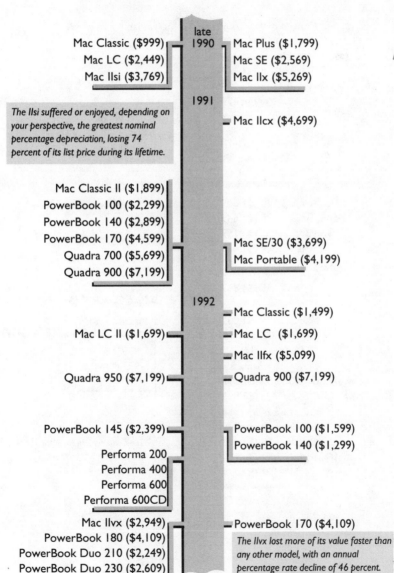

Introduced (Intro Price)		Discontinued (Exit Price)
Mac Classic ($999)	**late 1990**	Mac Plus ($1,799)
Mac LC ($2,449)		Mac SE ($2,569)
Mac IIsi ($3,769)		Mac IIx ($5,269)
	1991	
		Mac IIcx ($4,699)

The IIsi suffered or enjoyed, depending on your perspective, the greatest nominal percentage depreciation, losing 74 percent of its list price during its lifetime.

Introduced		Discontinued
Mac Classic II ($1,899)		
PowerBook 100 ($2,299)		
PowerBook 140 ($2,899)		
PowerBook 170 ($4,599)		Mac SE/30 ($3,699)
Quadra 700 ($5,699)		Mac Portable ($4,199)
Quadra 900 ($7,199)		
	1992	
		Mac Classic ($1,499)
Mac LC II ($1,699)		Mac LC ($1,699)
		Mac IIfx ($5,099)
Quadra 950 ($7,199)		Quadra 900 ($7,199)
PowerBook 145 ($2,399)		PowerBook 100 ($1,599)
		PowerBook 140 ($1,299)
Performa 200		
Performa 400		
Performa 600		
Performa 600CD		
Mac IIvx ($2,949)		PowerBook 170 ($4,109)
PowerBook 180 ($4,109)		
PowerBook Duo 210 ($2,249)		
PowerBook Duo 230 ($2,609)		

The IIvx lost more of its value faster than any other model, with an annual percentage rate decline of 46 percent.

139

Intro and Exit Timeline

Introduced (Intro Price) | **Discontinued (Exit Price)**

1993

Introduced (Intro Price):

Centris 610 ($1,859)
Centris 650 ($2,699)
Mac Color Classic ($1,389)
Mac LC III ($1,349)
PowerBook 165c ($3,399)
Quadra 800 ($4,679)

Performa 405/410
Performa 430
Performa 450

Mac LC 520 ($1,509)
PowerBook 145B ($1,649)
PowerBook 180c ($4,159)
Centris 660AV ($2,489)
Quadra 840AV ($4,069)

PowerBook 165 ($1,969)

Mac LC 475 ($1,082)
Performa 460/466/467
Performa 475/476
Performa 550
PowerBook Duo 250 ($2,599)
PowerBook Duo 270c ($3,099)
Quadra 605 ($969)
Quadra 610 ($1,439)
Quadra 650 ($2,399)
Quadra 660AV ($2,289)
Mac TV ($2,079)

Discontinued (Exit Price):

Mac IIci ($2,539)

Mac IIsi ($969)
Mac LC II ($1,239)
Qaudra 700 ($4,219)

PowerBook 145 ($2,149)

Mac Classic II ($1,079)

Mac IIvx ($1,659)
PowerBook Duo 210 ($1,499)
Centris 610
Centris 650
Centris 660AV

The Centris 660AV had the shortest lifespan of any model: 64 days.

The Quadra 605 is the least expensive model ever sold.

Intro and Exit Timeline

Introduced (Intro Price)   **Discontinued (Exit Price)**

1994

Performa 560

Mac LC 550 ($1,199)   Mac LC 520

Mac LC 575 ($1,699)

Power Mac 6100/60 ($1,819)   Quadra 800

Power Mac 7100/66 ($2,899)

Power Mac 8100/80 ($4,249)

Performa 575/577/578

PowerBook 520 ($2,269)   PowerBook 180

PowerBook 520c ($2,899)   PowerBook 165c

PowerBook 540 ($3,159)   PowerBook 180c

PowerBook 540c ($4,839)   PowerBook Duo 250

PowerBook Duo 280 ($2,639)   PowerBook Duo 270c

PowerBook Duo 280c ($3,759)

The historical average lifespan of discontinued Mac models is 548 days, but thanks to an accelerated product introduction pace, the average for models released in 1993 was just 251 days.

141

Billion-Dollar Bill and His Amazing American Express Card

Back in 1986, T/Maker published the popular WriteNow word processor for the Macintosh and was locked in a battle for market share with Microsoft Word. Although their companies were fierce competitors, T/Maker president J. A. Heidi Roizen and Microsoft chairman Bill Gates were good enough friends for Roizen to jokingly suggest that Gates simply buy her out.

Courtesy of Microsoft Corp.

Bill Gates, Microsoft chairman

After visiting Roizen's house one night prior to giving a speech in Silicon Valley, Gates accidentally left his wallet on the coffee table. Seizing the opportunity to play a practical joke, Roizen took Gates' American Express card to the T/Maker office in Mountain View where she promptly ran it through the company's credit card imprinter and filled out the sales slip for "one software company" at a purchase price of a cool $2 million.

Courtesy of T/Maker Co. and Microsoft Corp.

T/Maker president Heidi Roizen "sold" her company to Bill Gates.

When Roizen returned the wallet to Gates at a meeting later that day, the boy billionaire took one look at the American Express slip and exclaimed, "Hey, you overcharged me!"

In retrospect, it was probably a fair price. T/Maker sold WriteNow to WordStar in March of 1993 for an undisclosed sum, but still managed to sell almost $9 million worth of ClickArt during the year. And in June of 1994, T/Maker agreed to a buy-out offer from Deluxe Corporation, the terms of which remain confidential.

Lemmings: Why 1985 Wasn't Like 1984

In late 1984, Apple didn't have a stunning new product up its sleeve like it had the year before with Macintosh, so it tried to manufacture some excitement over The Macintosh Office, which was essentially the concept of connecting a group of Macs to a LaserWriter and sharing information using a device called a file server. There was only one small problem: the file server, a key component, was nowhere near ready to ship. To his credit, Jean-Louis

Courtesy of Apple Computer, Inc.

The Macintosh Office connected Macs with LaserWriters and a non-existent file server.

145

Gassée, then general manager of Apple France, refused to foist this charade upon his countrymen, not-so-secretly referring to it as "The Macintosh Orifice." Although Apple would not ship a file server until 1987, that didn't stop it from promoting The Macintosh Office in the United States in 1985.

Referring to the lack of a server, Jean-Louis Gassée called it "The Macintosh Orifice."

Trying to recreate the magic of the phenomenal *1984* commercial, Apple again turned to the creative team at its advertising agency to whip up something great for the upcoming Super Bowl XIX. Chiat/Day wanted to hire Ridley Scott, who directed *1984*, but he wasn't available, so his brother Tony was hired instead.

The result was a dark, 60-second commercial called *Lemmings*, in which long lines of blindfolded business

people, each with a hand upon the shoulder of the person ahead and briefcase in the other hand, trudge off the edge of a cliff like lemmings to the sea. Finally, the last man in the first line, presumably a Macintosh convert, lifts his blindfold and stops at the brink instead of plunging to his death.

Tony Scott reportedly found fault with the clouds over England and flew to Sweden to find just the right clouds to include in the commercial's background.

Courtesy of Apple Computer, Inc.

Lemmings likened DOS users to mindless rodents committing mass suicide.

147

Needless to say, *Lemmings* wasn't your typical commercial. It was thought-provoking, but it lacked the liberating appeal of *1984*. In fact, John Sculley hated it, and in a repeat of the prior year, ordered Chiat/Day to sell back the $1 million Super Bowl slot to ABC, which it managed to do. The creative team at Chiat/Day mounted an intense lobbying effort to get Sculley to reverse his decision, reminding him that Apple disliked *1984*, and that turned out to be a triumph.

Even though he was convinced he had done good work, copywriter Steve Hayden cautioned Apple, "You're going to bite the karmic weenie if you run *Lemmings* and can't deliver The [Macintosh] Office." Sculley left the decision up to marketing manager Mike Murray, who crossed his fingers and went for broke.

Courtesy of BBDO

Copywriter Steve Hayden warned of biting "the karmic weenie."

Chiat/Day was able to repurchase Apple's one minute of air time at a reduced price of $900,000 (what a bargain!), and the commercial ran in the fourth quarter of Super Bowl XIX on January 20, 1985. Although the San Francisco 49ers were well on their way to crushing the Miami Dolphins 38 to 16, much of the country remained glued to the television because Apple had run teaser newspaper advertisements warning, "If you go to the bathroom during the fourth quarter, you'll be sorry." In retrospect, it was Apple that was sorry.

Steve Jobs and John Sculley had front row seats for the disaster as they were both watching the Super Bowl in person at Stanford Stadium. For this event, Apple had filled the notoriously-uncomfortable wooden stands with soft, logo-emblazoned cushions and set up a huge stadium screen. To prime the audience of 90,000, Apple ran *1984* on the screen to an enthusiastic response before the game started. But when *Lemmings* ran at half time, the crowd sat in stunned silence. Not a good sign.

The commercial was supposed to convince the television audience of 43 million that The Macintosh Office offered liberation from the traditional, accepted ways of doing business (i.e., buying IBM PCs), but it managed instead to insult the very people it was trying to win over. By most accounts, *Lemmings* failed. Miserably.

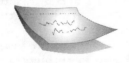

Responding to all of the negative fall-out, Mike Murray suggested running a public apology in *The Wall Street Journal*. Jay Chiat threatened that if Murray placed such an ad, Chiat/Day would buy the opposite page and apologize for the apology. The idea was dropped.

It's easy to look back and blame the *Lemmings* commercial for Apple's subsequent market troubles, but "you can't write a check with advertising that the product can't cash," emphasizes Hayden. "The fact that the file server was an empty plastic box might have something to do with the failure of The Macintosh Office." True enough. Imagine for a moment, if you will, that *Lemmings*, not *1984*, was used to introduce Macintosh. The commercial might very well have been favorably received because Apple could back it up with an extraordinary breakthrough product. Unfortunately, that was not the case and *Lemmings* goes down in history as proof that Apple was out of control and out of touch.

"This is the beginning of The Macintosh Office. I say beginning because this isn't going to be the 100 days of The Macintosh Office. It's going to take us two years to earn our way into the office."

Steve Jobs at the January 23, 1985 shareholders' meeting. (Was he inadvertently letting it slip that the file server would take two years to complete?)

Killer Rabbits on the Rampage

AppleShare 3.0 was code-named Killer Rabbit, after the blood-sucking character from the movie *Monty Python and the Holy Grail*. Although it was renamed before release, vestiges of its former incarnation can be found in the shipping version. If you have ever had File Sharing activated under System 7, look inside the File Sharing folder in the Preferences folder in the System folder.

Normally, the Mac writes an invisible PDS (Parallel Data Structure) file to each volume that is mounted while file sharing is on. However, in the cases of write-protected or read-only volumes (such as CD-ROMs), the Mac writes visible PDF files to the startup disk. These files are used to help manage file sharing and they have an icon of a Killer Rabbit. Incidentally, the Killer Rabbit is stored as ICN# resource 20002 in the File Sharing Extension file (this file's creator code is hhgg, which some say stands for Douglas Adams' book, *The Hitchhiker's Guide to the Galaxy*).

Looney Licenses

Ever read that itty-bitty, shrink-wrap license agreement that comes with most software packages? Usually they are boilerplate, weasel-like disclaimers absolving the publisher from any and all responsibility written by lawyers who have never used a computer. But every once in a while it pays to read the fine print. Consider, if you will, the complete text of HavenTree Software's licensing agreement for its EasyFlow flow-chart application, as well as some choice stuff taken from the license agreement used by House Industries, publisher of fine PostScript fonts.

"Steve [Jobs] will use anybody to his own advantage. He will say one thing and anybody who heard it would think that he was saying 'Maybe yes' or 'Maybe no.' You could never tell what he was thinking."

Steve Wozniak
Accidental Millionaire, p. 75

HavenTree's Bloodthirsty License Agreement

This is where the bloodthirsty license agreement is supposed to go explaining that EasyFlow is a copyrighted package sternly warning you not to pirate copies of it and explaining, in detail, the gory consequence if you do.

We know that you are an honest person, and are not going to go around pirating copies of EasyFlow; this is just as well with us since we worked hard to perfect it and selling copies of it is our only method of making anything out of all the hard work. For your convenience, EasyFlow is distributed on a non copy-protected diskette and you are free to do what you want with it (make backups, move from machine to machine, etc.) provided that it is never in use by more than one person at a time.

If, on the other hand, you are one of those few people who do go around pirating copies of software, you probably aren't going to pay much attention to a license agreement, bloodthirsty or not. Just keep your doors locked and look out for the HavenTree attack shark.

Honest Disclaimer

We don't claim EasyFlow is good for anything—if you think it is, great, but it's up to you to decide. If EasyFlow doesn't work, tough. If you lose a million because

153

EasyFlow messes up, it's you that's out the million, not us. If you don't like this disclaimer, tough. We reserve the right to do the absolute minimum provided by law, up to and including nothing.

This is basically the same disclaimer that comes with all software packages, but ours is in plain English and theirs is in legalese.

We didn't really want to include any disclaimer at all, but our lawyers insisted. We tried to ignore them but they threatened us with the attack shark (see license agreement above) at which point we relented.

House Industries
End User Agreement

Here's the long license agreement. You probably won't read it, but by opening this envelope you are agreeing to its terms. We'd like to remind you that these typefaces are the result of a lot of hard work and it would be really lame if they were haphazardly given out to anyone and everyone. If you don't agree with the terms, please return this envelope unopened to House Industries...[The agreement launches into the typical, verbose legal gobbledygook for a while, but then gets good again with points 5 and 6.]

5. **DESIGN** The user shall not knowingly or wantonly use House Industries products in bad taste or in poor design. Any and all uses of House Industries products in the above-stated manner will be punishable with fifty (50) lashes with a long metal ruler. These punishments/penalties will be carried out by a contracted security firm within thirty (30) days of the infraction. If the infraction is not punished within thirty (30) days of said infraction, all is forgiven and you will be placed on indefinite design probation.

6. **VIOLATION OF RULES** Any violation of the above rules would really suck and will make it very hard for small foundries such as House Industries to continue to crank out unique typography and cool artwork.

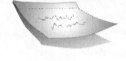

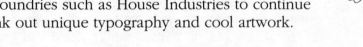

Jobs set the list price of the original Apple I at $666.66 by doubling the cost of manufacturing, which still allowed dealers a 33.3 percent markup on the wholesale price of $500. Fundamentalist Christians were quick to complain that 666 was the "mark of the beast." Jobs blew these people off with a concocted story about how he had taken the mystical number seven, subtracted one, another mystical number, to arrive at what he believed was a perfectly innocent price. Actually, Jobs wanted to charge $777, but Woz insisted that was too much.

The Remarkable Rise and Fabulous Fall of John Sculley

If you're a Macintosh true believer, you probably remember John Sculley as the man who ripped the heart out of Apple when he dethroned its folk hero founder, Steve Jobs. If you're an investor, you probably remember him as the shrewd businessman who guided and grew Apple through its most difficult years only to suffer the same fate he visited upon Jobs. Neither depiction is entirely fair, nor entirely untrue. Sculley's ten-year reign at Apple was filled with promise and enthusiasm, intrigue and betrayal, recovery and triumph, anguish and irony.

When Mike Markkula came out of retirement to join Apple in 1976, he had hoped to help it grow, then bow out gracefully after a few years. However, in a corporate power shift in March 1981, Markkula reluctantly assumed the role of president from Mike Scott, and Jobs took Markkula's place as chairman. Now he was back in the thick of things, but only temporarily.

The search for a new chief executive began not long after Markkula was thrust into the presidency. Jobs wanted someone, unlike Scott, whom he could manipulate, and the board hoped to find an experienced executive who could help Apple manage its phenomenal growth.

They found their man in John Sculley, the highly regarded president of Pepsi-Cola USA, the beverage subsidiary of PepsiCo.

Courtesy of Apple Computer, Inc.
Photo by Tim Zimberoff

John Sculley came to Apple from Pepsi.

Among the people approached to become Apple's president was Admiral Bobby [Ray] Inman, deputy director of the CIA until June 1982. But Inman concluded, "They needed someone with a marketing background and I didn't have it." (*The Little Kingdom*, pp. 318-319)

After 18 months of wooing, Sculley was named president and CEO of Apple on April 8, 1983. Sculley likes to tell people that what attracted him to Apple was the intellectual challenge of changing the world, but something as banal as money may have had a tiny little bit to do with his decision to hop from one coast to the other. To lure him away from his $500,000-a-year job at Pepsi, Apple granted him $1 million in annual pay (half salary, half bonus), a $1 million signing bonus, a $1 million golden parachute clause, options on 350,000 shares of Apple stock, and the difference in cost to buy a home in California equivalent to the one he owned in Connecticut.

When he moved to California in 1983, Sculley purchased a $1.9 million, 63-year old, five-bedroom English Tudor house at 1224 Cañada Road in the tony community of Woodside. Sculley renamed it the Blackburn Valley Morgan compound; Blackburn being a Sculley family name and Morgan the type of horse his third wife Leezy (Lee Adams) liked to raise.

"Do you want to spend the rest of your life selling sugared water or do you want a chance to change the world?"

Steve Jobs,
trying to con-
vince Sculley to
quit Pepsi and
join Apple
Odyssey, p. 90

> **"Think of Silicon Valley as Florence in the Renaissance. It's the place where anybody who is excited about doing something to change the world wants to be."**
>
> **Gerry Roche**, Heidrick & Struggles headhunter, pushing Sculley to accept Apple's offer
>
> *Playboy*, September 1987, p. 54

> "One thing that impressed me about Apple was that while the popular image was of two young boys starting a company, it was actually backed by one of the most sophisticated, experienced boards of directors you could find."
>
> **John Sculley**
> *Playboy*, September 1987, p. 54

For a while, things seemed to be going quite well for Sculley. He got on board just in time to ride the euphoric wave that was the Macintosh introduction, and he got along famously with Jobs, no small accomplishment that. Sculley and Jobs shared a symbiotic professional relationship. Sculley viewed himself as Jobs' marketing and management mentor, whereas Jobs was Sculley's technology tutor. During the good times of 1983 and 1984, the two were inseparable, often referred to as "the dynamic duo" in the business press. But the good times didn't last.

Following the successful introduction of the Macintosh in January 1984, Apple was feeling confident. Jobs and Sculley went for broke and built up a massive inventory for the Christmas season, but the demand never materialized and Apple found itself sitting on a pile of unsold computers. Tensions ran high at Apple because the company was facing serious trouble for the first time in its history. In the past, whatever mistakes Apple made (such as the Apple III and Lisa) were more than offset by the continued success of the Apple II. Things were different now because the entire industry had suffered a slump and the Apple II wasn't strong enough to carry the company by itself.

> **"I've made a lot of decisions in my life, but never one that changed my life more, never one that I felt better about, than coming to Apple. It isn't working for a company; it's a chance to work with people who were part of shaping history."**
>
> John Sculley, upon his one-year anniversary at Apple
>
> *Odyssey*, p. 198

John Sculley and Steve Jobs in happier times.

"Steve [Jobs] was nothing short of exciting. He was arrogant, outrageous, intense, demanding—a perfectionist. He was also immature, fragile, sensitive, vulnerable. He was dynamic, visionary, charismatic, yet often stubborn, uncompromising, and downright impossible."

John Sculley,
demonstrating
his mastery of
adjectives
Odyssey, p. 157

When times get tough, the tough get going, and it became apparent to the tough-minded executives at Apple that Jobs was more of a liability than an asset. Not content to restrict himself to the role of product visionary of his Macintosh division, Jobs was playing manager, meddling in areas of the company over which he had no jurisdiction. Step on enough toes, and they'll soon be kicking your ass, which is exactly what happened to Jobs. During a marathon board meeting which started on April 10, 1985, and continued for several hours the next day, Sculley threatened to resign if the board didn't back him on his decision to remove Jobs as executive vice president and general manager of the Macintosh division. The board agreed to strip Jobs of any operating role in the company, but allowed him to remain chairman. Sculley, who genuinely liked Jobs, didn't act right away, hoping to make a smooth transition. Mistake. Big mistake.

> **"Some naysayers claim the partnership will never last—that intense, mercurial Jobs, who owns nearly 12% of Apple stock (worth almost $200 million at current prices), will drive intense, focused Sculley back East."**
>
> *Fortune*
> February 20, 1984, p. 100

Less than a month later, on the eve of a trip to China where he would speak to the vice premier about using computers in education, Sculley was informed by Jean-Louis Gassée that Jobs planned to overthrow him during his absence. Sculley immediately canceled the trip and convened an emergency meeting of the company's

executive staff the very next day, May 24. When Sculley confronted Jobs with the coup rumor, Jobs lashed back, "I think you're bad for Apple and I think you're the wrong person to run this company." (*Odyssey*, p. 251)

Stung by Jobs' vicious attack, Sculley asked each executive to choose sides. One by one they fell in line behind Sculley and Jobs stalked out of the room. Even with this clear show of support, Sculley contemplated resigning, but changed his mind after a good night's rest. Two days after the meeting, Jobs had the temerity to suggest that Sculley become chairman and that he be appointed president and chief executive officer. Sorry, Charlie, but Sculley didn't play that game. On May 31, a week after the explosive executive meeting, Sculley signed the paperwork that stripped Jobs of all operational responsibilities. He retained the figurehead title of chairman and was put in charge of "global thinking" in a remote office dubbed Siberia. Jobs, the founder, had been hoisted on his own petard, Sculley the outsider.

> **"I had given Steve greater power than he had ever had and I had created a monster."**
>
> John Sculley
>
> *Odyssey*, p. 240

Just as he vowed to exact his revenge after Scott had taken the Lisa away from him, Jobs began thinking of ways to get back at Sculley and Apple. On September 12, Jobs told the board of directors that he and a few "low level" employees planned to start an unnamed company that would address the needs of higher education, and he asked if Apple would be interested in licensing Macintosh software to him. He assured the board that his new venture would complement Apple, not compete with it, but offered to resign as chairman nonetheless. The board refused to accept the resignation, asking him to defer the move for a week as it contemplated the possibility of buying as much as 10 percent of the new venture. At a 7:25 A.M. meeting the next day, Friday the 13th, Jobs presented Sculley with a list of the five employees he was taking with him: Susan Barnes (senior controller for U.S. sales and marketing), George Crow (engineering manager), Dan'l Lewin (higher education marketing manager), Rich Page (Apple Fellow), and Bud Tribble (manager of software engineering).

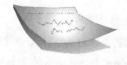

As chairman of the board, Jobs had little to do on a day-to-day basis, so he tried convincing the National Aeronautics and Space Administration to allow him to fly on the space shuttle as a private citizen. Fortunately for Jobs, NASA turned him down. On January 28, 1986, less than two minutes into its tenth flight, the space shuttle Challenger exploded in a terrible fireball, killing all seven crew members.

Sculley was incensed. These employees were privy to sensitive data on the Big Mac project Apple had underway (also known as 3M because it would have a 17-inch, million-pixel display, a million megabytes of memory, and run a million instructions per second with a 68020 processor and Unix software). Feeling that Jobs had crossed over the line, the executive staff discussed the possibility of removing Jobs as chairman, but Jobs beat them to the punch. On September 17, Jobs officially resigned, but instead of quietly tendering his resignation to Markkula, he also sent copies to the press in an obvious attempt to

provoke a sympathetic reaction from the public. The public responded alright, but not the way he imagined; the news of Jobs' departure sent Apple stock up a full point that day.

Steve Jobs' Resignation Letter

This is a verbatim copy of the resignation letter sent by chairman Steve Jobs to company vice chairman Mike Markkula.

September 17, 1985

Mr. A.C. Markkula Jr.
Apple Computer Inc.
10495 Bandley Drive
Cupertino, CA 95014

Dear Mike:

This morning's papers carried suggestions that Apple is considering removing me as Chairman. I don't know the source of these reports but they are both misleading to the public and unfair to me.

You will recall that at last Thursday's Board meeting I stated I had decided to start a new venture and I tendered my resignation as Chairman.

The Board declined to accept my resignation and asked me to defer it for a week. I agreed to do so in light of the encouragement the Board offered with regard to the proposed new venture and the indications that Apple would invest in it. On Friday, after I told John Sculley who would be joining me, he confirmed Apple's willingness to discuss areas of possible collaboration between Apple and my new venture.

Subsequently the Company appears to be adopting a hostile posture toward me and the new venture. Accordingly, I must insist upon the immediate acceptance of my resignation. I would hope that in any public statement it feels it must issue, the company will make it clear that the decision to resign as Chairman was mine.

I find myself both saddened and perplexed by the management's conduct in this matter which seems to me contrary to Apple's best interest. Those interests remain a matter of deep concern to me, both because of my past association with Apple and the substantial investment I retain in it.

I continue to hope that calmer voices within the Company may yet be heard. Some Company representatives have said they fear I will use proprietary Apple technology in my new venture. There is no basis for any such concern. If that concern is the real source of Apple's hostility to the venture, I can allay it.

As you know, the company's recent reorganization left me with no work to do and no access even to regular management reports. I am but 30 and want still to contribute and achieve.

After what we have accomplished together, I would wish our parting to be both amicable and dignified.

Yours sincerely,

Steven Jobs

Steven P. Jobs.

166

Jobs' resignation didn't appease Apple. On September 23, the company filed a suit against Jobs and Page, enjoining them from using any proprietary information and charging Jobs with dereliction of his duties as chairman. In retrospect, the suit was ludicrous. While at Apple, Jobs was considered an incompetent manager with little technical skill, but once he departs he suddenly becomes a major threat to the well-being of Apple? Come on! Realizing the suit served only to give Jobs credibility, Apple quietly settled out of court in January of 1986.

> "It is hard to think that a $2 billion company with 4,300-plus people couldn't compete with six people in blue jeans."
>
> **Steve Jobs**, on Apple's suit following his resignation
> *Newsweek*, September 30, 1985, p. 57

With Jobs out of the way, Sculley led Apple through its most prosperous times, helping grow the business from $600 million in net sales when he joined in 1983 to almost $8 billion a decade later. Along the way, he picked up an interest in politics and stumped for Bill Clinton, who was rumored to have eliminated Sculley as his running mate only because he was twice divorced. After Clinton's 1992 election, Sculley was asked to join the new cabinet, but he declined. He also turned down top jobs at American Express and IBM, both of which were facing hard times. He'd soon regret not jumping at those opportunities.

> **"[Sculley] took a bunch of computer hackers who run around in sandals and jeans and married them to Wall Street. It takes a smart human being to marry cultures like that."**
>
> **Andrew Seybold**, editor
> of *Outlook on Mobile Computing*
>
> *Worth*, May 1994, p. 87

Apple's earnings per share peaked at $4.33 in fiscal year 1992, only to collapse to 73¢ per share the following year on deteriorating gross margins inflicted by fierce price competition. The board of directors had lost faith in Sculley and on June 18, 1993, he stepped down as CEO and was replaced by Michael "Diesel" Spindler, president, COO, and board member. Like Jobs in 1985, Sculley retained the title of chairman and was supposed to focus on emerging new business opportunities for Apple. Like Jobs, he found the figurehead role odious and began planning his exit.

Courtesy of Apple Computer, Inc.
Photo by William Mosgrove

Mike Spindler replaced Sculley as CEO in 1993.

On October 1, 1993, at his four-acre estate in Greenwich, Connecticut, Sculley held a five-hour meeting with Peter Caserta, president of Spectrum Information Technologies of Manhasset, New York. Caserta demonstrated his company's AXCELL cellular modem working with one of Sculley's pet products, the much-maligned Newton MessagePad. Sculley was so impressed with the technology and the portfolio of patents held by Spectrum that he failed to adequately investigate Caserta's shady past when offered the reins of the $100-million, 38-person company.

"I've had some wonderful years at Pepsi, an extraordinary journey at Apple, and now I am ready to head off to new challenges. I'm tremendously grateful for the support of so many phenomenal Apple people. I wish everyone involved with Apple great success in the years ahead. I'll be out there cheering you all on."

John Sculley,
upon resigning
from Apple

On October 15, the day after Apple posted a 97 percent drop in earnings for its fourth quarter, Sculley played the sacrificial lamb, resigning his position as Apple's chairman and taking with him $1 million in severance pay, a one-year consulting fee of $750,000, plus a commitment from Apple to buy his Woodside mansion and Leer 55 jet.

Just three days later, Sculley shocked the business world with his announcement that he was joining Spectrum as chairman and CEO at a salary of $1 million with options to purchase 18 million shares (20 percent of the firm's outstanding common stock). It wasn't his compensation that raised eyebrows, it was the company he was joining.

Spectrum was embroiled in a class-action shareholders' lawsuit pertaining to inflated revenue projections made by Caserta in May, and the Securities and Exchange Commission was investigating charges of stock manipulation. Furthermore, Spectrum engaged in aggressive accounting practices that made it look much more profitable than it really was. Although Sculley claims he didn't know the full story when he accepted his position at Spectrum, he was smart enough to realize that he had

> **"Technology gives you a good reason not to take anything on faith. Suddenly there is so much information you can almost effortlessly find the facts for yourself. You can test your ideas and explore alternatives. Computing offers you every incentive to become skeptical."**
>
> John Sculley, spouting advice he failed to follow with Spectrum
>
> *Odyssey,* p. 151

stepped in it but good. He began looking for an escape hatch, and on February 7, 1994, he resigned from Spectrum and filed a $10 million suit against Caserta, claiming he failed to reveal the SEC probe and Spectrum's accounting practices in an attempt to dupe Sculley into joining the firm so that Caserta could dump his stock at inflated prices. Spectrum promptly turned around and sued Sculley for $300 million, charging him with breach of contract, mismanagement, and theft of trade secrets. In March, both parties withdrew their lawsuits, but by then Sculley's reputation in the business community had been irreparably soiled.

"Apple is an Ellis Island company. Apple is built on refugees from other companies. These are the extremely bright individual contributors who were troublemakers at other companies."

Steve Jobs
Playboy, February 1985,
p. 58

Sculley Timeline

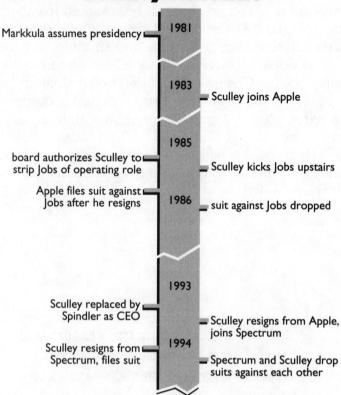

Markkula assumes presidency — **1981**

1983 — Sculley joins Apple

1985

board authorizes Sculley to
strip Jobs of operating role — — Sculley kicks Jobs upstairs

Apple files suit against
Jobs after he resigns — **1986** — suit against Jobs dropped

1993

Sculley replaced by
Spindler as CEO —

— Sculley resigns from Apple,
joins Spectrum

Sculley resigns from
Spectrum, files suit — **1994** — Spectrum and Sculley drop
suits against each other

Stupid Mac Stories

No doubt about it, of all the computers on the market, the Mac is the easiest to use. However, that doesn't mean that it's so easy to use that anybody can do it. As technical support representatives know all too well, "Nothing is ever foolproof, because fools are so ingenious." If you've been around the computer industry long enough, surely you have heard the urban legend about the temporary employee who tried to correct word processing mistakes by applying Liquid Paper to the computer screen. Then there's the one about the secretary who was asked to duplicate some floppy disks, only to return with Xerox copies. While these examples are almost surely apocryphal, all of the following stories are based upon actual reports of Macintosh stupidity. Only the names have been changed to protect the incredibly ignorant.

Why Mouse Pads Were Invented

"I train college students how to use Macs. One day, I was talking about the use of the mouse, explaining the concepts of pointing and clicking, etc., when I heard some tittering behind my back. There was a girl pointing and clicking away like mad, while she was rolling the mouse all over the monitor screen!"—Scott L. Foglesong

"Once I was giving instructions over the phone for some program or another. I told the person to 'Type your name and a Return.' He enters his name no problem, but then I hear him spelling out loud 'R-E-T...' as he hunts and pecks his way around the keyboard."

Tom Petaccia

Why Windex Was Invented

"I recall someone calling me when they were having problems with a cursor that wouldn't move. It seems this person was trying to move the cursor by pointing on the screen...with his fingers."—Chris Gordon

How the Trackball Was Invented

"I had a client who never used a mouse before. We installed his Mac and gave some quick instructions on how to use it. After about three weeks, I had not heard anything from him, so I stopped by on one of my regular visits. I was amazed to find out he had developed all the skills needed to operate the computer. The trait that amazed me the most is that he would pick up the mouse, turn it over and roll the ball around with his thumb. It actually worked and it took us months to break him of this habit!"—Walter E. Craven

"I know a guy who uses his mouse 180° backwards. Seems the person who set up the Mac had inadvertently left the mouse positioned with the cord coming out the front and the hapless new Mac user simply assumed that's the way it's supposed to work. So he drags it towards him to move the cursor up (like a flight stick in a plane), right to go left, and vice versa!"

Mike Cecere

How Not to Replace Mouse Balls

"I had a salesman come into the technical area once with a request from a client for 'mouse balls' and he had no idea what these were. So instead of explaining to him what they were, we bought a mouse trap, and left it on his desk with a note reading 'Please bait this trap and leave it in the back room. As soon as we catch a mouse we can fill your client's order.' Being the good salesman he was, he baited it and set the trap! I hated to explain that it was a joke, but we had to!"—Walter E. Craven

Remote Control Macintosh

"I used to work for a Macintosh dealer in London. We had a guy who had never used a computer before come in for a demo of the Macintosh II. The salesman sat him down, got him coffee, then went to pick up some brochures. As he walked back into the showroom, he was amused to see the customer standing facing the Mac, mouse in hand (two feet off the desk) pointing and clicking madly at the screen thinking it was some kind of remote control."—Rory Choudhuri

"We once got a call from an elderly woman whose son had decided it would be great to give her a Mac, so she could easily write letters to him. Figuring the Mac had such an easy interface that she'd have no trouble, he set it all up for her and then went on his way. Soon afterward, she called us for help. She couldn't seem to type more than the beginning of a letter, when the machine just froze up. We walked her step-by-step through everything she was doing to figure out what the problem was. Her son had told her to click on the word processor's icon to launch the application, then type her letter, save it, etc. Well, she'd done as instructed. But she only clicked once on the word processor's icon. So as she began to type, she was actually renaming the application something like 'Dear John, How have you been do...'"

Mike Nugent

Runaway Mouse

"When my wife first got her Mac, she ran her mouse up against a bookcase at the end of her desk. Needing to go further to the right, she moved her mouse up the side of the bookcase, and then complained what a dumb idea the mouse was."—Andrew Tarshis

I Can See Clearly Now

"One of our customers was using Photoshop and we explained, in passing, that she could use the magnifying glass tool to see more details in her image. The next time we visited her, she had put a real, king-size magnifying glass on a stand in front of her screen."—Roland Mailleux

I Can See Clearly Now, the Sequel

"One of our customers kept encountering an error when trying to print. The Mac would present an alert box saying 'Looking for LaserWriter,' then it would finally give up, reporting that the 'Printer could not be found.' Obviously, the printer was either not turned on or incorrectly connected to the network. But this person tried to remedy the situation by turning the Mac to face the LaserWriter so that it could see it, as if these things had infrared connections!"—Scott Harris

"A lot of programs present some sort of splash screen upon launching. Usually this displays the name of the program, the publisher, and copyright information. To bypass the screen and get on with using the program, the documentation often instructs the user to press any key. Apparently even this seemingly simple instruction is way over the heads of some folks, who end up calling technical support asking them where the 'any' key is located on their keyboards."

Ron Contarino

Installation Is a Breeze

"A woman called for help in installing our software on her hard drive. I told her to insert the disk. She said that she had. I told her to double-click the disk icon. She said she did. Then I told her how to install the software, etc. She said she did. I wanted to make sure she could see the Finder's desktop, so I told her to close the window. There was a moment of silence. The woman then said that she had just closed her bedroom window, but she wasn't sure how that was going to help."—Robin Lane

179

"A friend of mine works in technical support for Salient Software, developers of DiskDoubler [a utility for increasing the amount of disk space through compression]. A customer called in complaining, 'DiskDoubler doesn't work.' So my friend asked, 'Is the DD Menu in the your menu bar?' to which the customer replied, 'No.' Hoping to direct the customer to a helpful page in the documentation, my friend inquired, 'OK, do you have the manual?' At this point my friend hears that sound of packaging being opened in the background. The customer had thought that all she needed to do was put the DiskDoubler box next to her hard drive, and that would double her disk space."

Greg Dougherty

Where There's a Will, There's a Way

"The owner of a type shop I worked for years ago came in with a print job saved on an IBM 5.25-inch disk and asked if we could read it. I pointed to the Mac's small floppy slot and told him the data must be transferred to a 3.5-inch disk for use on the Mac. He thought about it for a moment, and then asked if we couldn't just trim the disk. With scissors!"—Geoff Latta

If It Don't Fit, Force It

"One of my clients called complaining of a problem with his floppy drive. He inserted a disk into the drive, but now the drive refused to eject the disk. I explained to him that he could insert a straightened-out paper clip into

"My friend knows a lady who bought a Mac on which she placed a pirated copy of WriteNow. Of course, she didn't read any manuals, nor run the Mac demo disk, but she managed to get everything to work. My friend visited her to check up on some minor problem. He noticed her extraordinarily tidy disk contained the System folder, WriteNow, and hardly anything else. No folders labeled Data, Letters, Pamphlets, Private, etc. The explanation was obvious as soon as she opened WriteNow to begin work. Instead of creating a new document, she opened an existing document, placed the cursor on the down scroll arrow, and depressed the mouse button. After a considerable amount of time had passed, she arrived at the bottom of her only document—where she kept all her writing— and started typing the new letter!"

Vegard Brenna

the little hole next to the drive slot to manually eject the disk. He tried and reported it was impossible. When he finally brought the Mac into my office for inspection, I found that he had stuffed a 5.25-inch floppy disk into the 3.5-inch drive by folding it in thirds."—Paul Retsis

Sticky Situation

"I once worked for a magazine at which all the floppies were stored in a metal filing cabinet. Then we discovered that someone had stuck so many memos to the cabinet using such powerful magnets that virtually every disk was bulk erased."—Louise Kohl Leahy

"I once took a technical support call from a customer who was complaining that our electronic bulletin board system wasn't working. 'What's the problem?,' I asked. He replied, 'Your BBS isn't sending me the file that I was told to download.' When I asked him the name of the terminal program that he was using, he responded, 'I'm just calling the number the guy told me to call and when I hear the squeal, I plug the line into the modem and it is not sending me my file!'"

Rusty Jackson

And the Worms Ate Into His Brain

"When Berkeley Systems' After Dark screen saver first came out, I installed it on a machine shared by two illustrators. I told one of them, but the other wasn't around. We had the worm-munching module on. When the other illustrator came in the next morning, he started up the machine, opened the drawing he had been working on for days in Aldus Freehand, and went to get a cup of coffee while it loaded. When he got back, the worms were chewing up the screen. He panicked. He came rushing up to me with this story of how he had a virus, but that he had immediately shut off the machine, and that he thought it had only nibbled a little around the edges of his drawing, but now he was terrified of starting up the machine again."—Andrew Tarshis

"A woman in my office had been using Microsoft Word on her Mac. Instead of choosing Open from the File menu, every single time she wanted to open a file she would quit Word, find the file in the Finder, and open it by double-clicking."

Joe Holmes

Quick, Call 911

"We had just recently installed a network of ten Macs in a national magazine's editorial department when one day we received a frantic call from the editor who breathlessly announced, 'I have a bomb on the screen. I've asked everybody to leave the room. What do I need to do next?'"—Roland Mailleux

"My company distributes membership data on CD-ROM. One unhappy recipient of the disc called complaining that the disc didn't work when he placed it in his stereo's CD player."

Mary McManigle

The Great Caffeine Conspiracy

As any self-respecting Mac programmer can tell you, Jolt Cola is the soft drink of choice for late-night coding sessions because, as the slogan goes, it's got "Twice the Caffeine, All the Taste." Caffeine is naturally present in coffee beans, tea leaves, cocoa beans, and kola nuts. Its bitter taste balances the sweet flavor in soft drinks, plus it has the pleasant side-effect of stimulating brain cells, helping reduce drowsiness and fatigue while improving concentration and speeding up reactions. So it's no surprise that software publishers have been known to stockpile massive quantities of Jolt and Hostess Twinkies to keep their programmers happy and productive during the crunch times that inevitably occur before shipping a new package.

But a little independent research has uncovered the true facts in what could be called The Great Caffeine Conspiracy (soon to be a major motion picture from director Oliver Stone). Just as malt liquor has considerably more alcohol than regular beer, Jolt contains much more caffeine than most sodas.

"**Soft drinks were never intended to be a health food, and we refuse to mask our 'product benefits' behind new fangled corn syrup or fruit juice additives. Jolt is a back to basics product. What surprises most...is Jolt has less calories than Pepsi. Yet our two hits of caffeine provide a burst of energy.**"

C. J. Rapp,
Jolt Company
president

Note: According to The Jolt Company's literature, Jolt Cola has three, count 'em, three fewer calories than Pepsi.

While it is true that Jolt has the highest level of caffeine for soft drinks allowed by the U.S. Food & Drug Administration, it's far from the most stimulating beverage legally available.

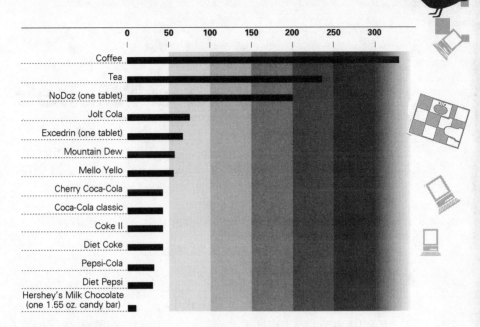

	0	50	100	150	200	250	300
Coffee							
Tea							
NoDoz (one tablet)							
Jolt Cola							
Excedrin (one tablet)							
Mountain Dew							
Mello Yello							
Cherry Coca-Cola							
Coca-Cola classic							
Coke II							
Diet Coke							
Pepsi-Cola							
Diet Pepsi							
Hershey's Milk Chocolate (one 1.55 oz. candy bar)							

This chart shows the milligrams of caffeine per 12 ounce serving, unless otherwise noted.

As the accompanying chart clearly demonstrates, ounce for ounce, a strong cup of coffee has five times the caffeine content of Jolt. (Caffeine content varies widely depending on bean variety and method of preparation. For example, drip brewing releases much more caffeine than percolating.) Even a spot of well-steeped tea is more than three times as powerful as Jolt. So the next time you want a little liquid lift-off, remember the facts, not the slogans.

The information for the caffeine chart was provided by Bristol-Myers Squibb, Coca-Cola USA, Hershey Chocolate USA, The Jolt Company, and Pepsi-Cola.

What's in a Name?

The true—and often bizarre—stories behind some of the most prominent and obscure company names in the Macintosh industry.

Abacus Concepts

Jim Gagnon and Dan Feldman began designing and coding their flagship data analysis product—StatView—in 1984 under the business name Eternal Rhythm Software. But when it came time to incorporate in 1985, they realized they would have to abandon that name. "People were telling us that it sounded like a digestive problem or a cult," laughs Feldman. "So, we did some brainstorming and tried to think of an instrument that symbolized graphical data analysis. The abacus was the perfect device. So, StatView on a Macintosh is just an extension of an Abacus Concept and hence our name."

ACIUS

Guy Kawasaki, former Apple evangelist and former president of ACIUS, likes to joke that ACIUS stands for "Apple Computer, Inc., Unshipped Software." That's because Kawasaki left Apple to publish an American version of 4th Dimension after Apple helped develop it in-house (under the code name Silver Surfer, after the favorite comic book character of author Laurent Ribardière) then refused to publish it in deference to pressure from Ashton-Tate, who was working on its own database program, dBASE Mac. In reality, the name of the French founding company is Analyses Conseils Informations (ACI), so it seemed only natural that the United States arm of the company be called ACIUS (pronounced Ace E Us). In November, 1992 the company changed its name to ACI US, Inc.

Adobe Systems

The company that developed the PostScript page-description language derives its name from Adobe Creek, located near the Los Altos Hills, California homes of founders Dr. John Warnock and Dr. Charles Geschke.

Advanced
GRAVIS

Advanced Gravis

This Canadian manufacturer of joysticks and game controllers was founded in the late 1970s by Grant Russell and Dennis Scott-Jackson, who were both studying Latin at the time. What, you might ask, does that have to do with anything? Well, a popular slang term back then was "heavy," as in "Wow man, that's a heavy concept!," and it just so happens that "gravis" is Latin for "heavy." So, do you dig this groovy little explanation, or what?

ALDUS®

Aldus

When Aldus president Paul Brainerd joined forces with four software engineers in 1984, their goal was to redefine the way people communicated. Their vision was embodied in PageMaker, the premiere desktop publishing package that allowed people to easily combine text and graphics on a page. "We faced many challenges in the early days, not the least of which was finding a name for our company. We were introducing a new form of publishing and in the process creating a new market. Our name needed to reflect that. We considered a hundred or more names, but nothing worked for us," recalls Brainerd. Eventually a reference librarian at the Oregon State University library in Corvallis located a book on the history of publishing that explained the contributions of

Aldus Manutius, a 15th-Century Renaissance printing pioneer who introduced the small book format, italicized type, and standardized punctuation. "The parallels were immediately evident," states Brainerd. "Like Aldus, we were basing our new approach to publishing on the recent technological advancements of our time. For us these were the microcomputer and the laser printer rather than the Gutenberg press."

Altsys

Although the company that developed Aldus FreeHand was founded in December 1984 in Jim Von Ehr's dining room, Altsys' origins go back much further than that. "I was sort of a hacker in college back in the computer Stone Age of the 1970s," admits Von Ehr. "A friend and I learned about the innards of the CDC 6500 operating system by hacking our way into the system source libraries on several occasions. This wasn't always appreciated by the powers that be; one time a kindly professor suggested I leave town for a week or two until things cooled off (thanks, Len!). I thought of us as the 'alternate systems programming group,' which I shortened to Altsys. I liked the name, and the connotation, so 10 years later I chose it for my company. Unfortunately, it has proven to be so hard for people to say that we test would-be receptionists for their ability to say it properly. We had a receptionist from a temp agency who never could say it right, even after a month of trying, so we had to replace her. I had hoped that our triangle logo, putting the 'Alt' inside, and the 'sys' outside, would make it more comprehensible. That doesn't seem to have happened..." Luckily for Von Ehr, nobody seems to have any problems whatsoever pronouncing Fontographer, the name of his most popular product today.

Ambrosia Software

Prolific shareware author Andrew Welch has a string of hits to his name, most recently the masterpiece arcade game Maelstrom, which is loosely based upon Asteroids. He had been distributing his wares under his own name for years, but has recently assumed a more professional identity. "As an avid reader of mythology, it was a natural that I would pick a mythos-related name for my new company," says Welch. "The Greek gods of yore towered among the heavens, looking down upon the Earth and man's futile writhings with amusement. Amidst their numerous feasts and celebrations, they drank nectar from the sweetest of flowers and ate a divine substance know as ambrosia. And from there comes Ambrosia Software."

Apple Computer

According to Steve Wozniak, it was Steve Jobs who thought up the name for the company one afternoon in early 1976 as the two drove along Highway 85, between Palo Alto and Los Altos. "Steve was still half involved with a group of friends who ran the commune-type All-One Farm in Oregon. And he would go up and work there for a few months before returning to the Bay Area. He had just come back from one of his trips and we were driving along and he said 'I've got a great name: Apple Computer.' Maybe he worked in Apple trees. I didn't even ask. Maybe it had some other meaning to him. Maybe the idea just occurred based upon Apple Corps [the Beatles' recording company]. He had been a musical person, like many technical people are. It might have sounded good partly because of that connotation. I thought instantly, 'We're going to have a lot of copyright problems.' But we didn't. Both of us tried to think of technical-sounding mixtures of words, like Executek and Matrix Electronics, but after ten minutes of trying, we both realized we weren't going to beat Apple Computer."

BAUDVILLE®

Baudville

"The word Baudville is a play on the words baud and vaudeville," says chairman Bill Darooge. "It was coined in 1983 while scanning the dictionary. I was looking for an alternative name to use in the event Xebec (an Arab trading vessel) did not pass the trademark search. In the early 1980s, modems were a hot new device for the micro market and I had been reading about modem transmission speed, hence the word baud was on the brain when I saw the word vaudeville in the dictionary. Out popped Baudville. As it happened, Xebec was already in use, so Baudville prevailed."

Brøderbund®

Brøderbund

This entertainment and productivity software company was founded over a decade ago by three brothers of Swedish descent: Don, Doug, and Gary Carlston. Doug had written a TRS-80 role-playing game called Galactic Revolution in which there was a merchant guild called Broderbund. When the three brothers decided to go into business selling software, they adopted the guild's name. But fearful that people might associate them with the similarly-named South African secret society, they used a diacritical mark which made the name more Swedish-sounding (pronounced brood er bund). And for their logo, they appropriated the three golden crowns from the Swedish national emblem, an appropriate symbol for three Swedish-American brothers.

CE SOFTWARE

CE Software

Back in 1981, president Dick Skeie ran a successful computer retail outlet in West Des Moines, Iowa, called Computer Emporium. His customers often needed custom programming, and to satisfy those needs Skeie contracted out to Don Brown, then a student at Drake University. After publishing Apple II programs for several years, they decided to jump to Mac development in 1985 so they borrowed the initials from the retail store and spun off a new company called CE Software, which went on to produce the popular QuicKeys and QuickMail packages.

CoStar

Kensington Microware founder Andrew Newmark left to start a new hardware company and wanted a name that described the interaction between the firm's gadgets and the computer user. "We picked CoStar from the film business. For example, Dustin Hoffman and Tom Cruise co-starred in the hit film *Rain Man*. In a similar way, we're trying to design products—such as the LabelWriter—that work together with you to make good things happen."

195

Dantz Development

In 1984, brothers Larry and Richard Zulch decided to create a company to take advantage of the opportunity the Macintosh presented. They didn't want a techie-sounding name that started with Micro, Super, Ultra, or whatever, or ended with Soft, Tech, Pro, Mac, etc. So Richard wrote a little program which generated all the possible combinations of a list of prefixes and suffixes they didn't like. Recalls Larry, "If a name appeared on the list, we wouldn't use it! It was amazing how many now-familiar names did appear: Microsoft, MicroPro, SuperMac, Microtech, etc. We then decided that we wanted a name at the beginning of the alphabet, one syllable, with useful connotations. We started at A. When we got to D, I said 'What about Dance? Dance connotes art and precision.' Richard replied, 'Good idea, but we can't have people thinking we're a dance troupe. How about spelling it Dantz? That gets a Z in there, as well.' Our last name is Zulch, and we've always had a certain fondness for Zs." And so, Dantz Development Corporation was founded in 1984 and its first product was the BoxBack for Iomega's 5-MB serial Bernoulli drive. Dantz has since gone on to capture a large portion of the backup software market with its popular Retrospect and DiskFit packages.

 Dayna

Dayna Communications, Inc.

Dayna was founded in 1984 by Bill Sadlier, Lynn Alley, and Steve Alley. In October of that year, Lynn Alley had just finished reading a story in *Byte* magazine about a funny new computer called Macintosh. He proposed that they create a product which would make the Macintosh capable of running DOS software. One year later, Dayna introduced a product to do just that: MacCharlie (IBM had been using Charlie Chaplin's "Little Tramp" character to push its PC line). Today, Dayna is best known for its full line of Ethernet connectivity products and is the second largest Macintosh Ethernet adapter manufacturer in the world. So where did this big, prestigious company get its name? From Bill Sadlier's little girl, Dayna, who was born in 1984, just like the Mac.

Delta Point.

DeltaPoint

When it comes to naming companies, no source of inspiration is too obscure or mundane. Case in point: DeltaPoint. Founded in May 1989 as part of a management buyout of the Macintosh division of Access Technology, DeltaPoint's first, and most popular product is DeltaGraph, a powerful graphing program. President & CEO, Ray Kingman, lets us in on the name's secret: "The name came from the index of functions in *Inside Macintosh* (page I-475). The Delta-Point function is a toolbox utility which subtracts the co-ordinates of point A from point B. There is no special meaning behind the function that applies to the company other than the fact that customers find it is easy to say and remember."

Delta Tao Software

Many people incorrectly assume that Delta Tao Software somehow evolved from Delta Tau Sigma, the CalTech fraternity of president Joe Williams. Setting the record straight once and for all, Williams explains that "Delta is the symbol used by engineers around the world to signify change. One would refer to Delta V to mean 'change in velocity.' I admit, this is engineerspeak, but forgive me for a minute. We're mostly engineers (if bit nerds pass for engineers), so this made sense. Tao (pronounced DOW) means 'the Path,' or 'the Way.' It's the big concept behind Taoism. We're mostly Taoists around here, so this made sense, too. Now, when you put these together, Delta Tao means 'The Changing Path.' We thought that this was almost a profound statement of direction, so we adopted it as a name." Leave it to a bunch of philosophical Taoist engineers to name their first product, an affordable color paint program for the Mac, ColorMacCheese.

Drew Pictures

Although Drew Pictures is now a highly-regarded developer of cutting-edge CD-ROM games such as Iron Helix (published by Spectrum Holobyte), it has humble beginnings. "The name was invented as a friend and I were walking down the street drinking coffee and discussing whether I should quit my job at Paracomp (publisher of Swivel 3D) and work as an independent producer," recalls Drew Huffman. "Of course, I'd need a company name. My last name didn't seem to work very well, but my first name was interesting because there is a sort of pun as to how I got started...I drew 3-D computer pictures. We thought of Drew Pictures as a sort of farcical reference to large motion picture companies like LucasFilms and Paramount Pictures."

❖ *Farallon*®

Farallon Computing

This networking-products company got its name from the Farallon Islands which are located 25 miles off the coast of San Francisco. President Reese Jones notes that Farallon is Spanish for "barren, rocky place," and is "almost unpronounceable in most east Asian languages." Jones likes that the islands are: an ecological sanctuary, the main breeding ground for the great white shark, a nuclear waste dump site, and a little closer to Japan than Silicon Valley. He also enjoys sailing around the islands which he can see from his home in the Berkeley Hills. The dots to the left of the name Farallon in the logo are supposed to represent the islands themselves.

FWB

Manufacturer of Hammer mass-storage devices, FWB represents the combined initials of founder Norman Fong and two of his friends who helped put the company together back in 1984: Will McDonald and Bob Johnson.

Inline Software

"An old friend of mine had gotten developer status with Apple and I was incredibly envious," admits Darryl Peck. "Turns out he just wanted to buy a Mac II at 50% off and did not care much about the other stuff. So, I got Apple to send me all the cool binders and technical info. It was like getting a great drug directly from Cupertino. One day Apple calls and informs us that to remain developers we must release a product. There was no way I was going to lose our status at that point, so we found another friend who was just about finished writing a cool HyperCard stack called Bomber. We convinced him to let us publish it." A few years earlier, Peck had founded a company

called Inline Design with the idea of opening a design firm in New York City, but that never got off the ground. "I figured I could save the $40 filing fee, so we decided to publish Bomber using the old company name. As you can see, I never really expected to start a large software publishing company. We finally changed our name to Inline Software to let people know what we *really* do for a living."

Kiwi SOFTWARE, Inc.

Kiwi SOFTWARE

Most people think that Kiwi SOFTWARE was named as such because its founder is from New Zealand. Actually, Yann Ricard is a Frenchman who got caught up in the excitement of the 1987 America's Cup raging in Freemantle, Australia. To regain the cup, the USA entered five yachts designed by some of the most prestigious aeronautics firms in the country. Still, tiny New Zealand's single challenger, the Kiwi Magic, beat out every other boat except the Stars and Stripes, which brought the cup back to San Diego. "Even though Kiwi Magic was defeated in the end, it showed that love and passion for what you do can help you overcome the handicap of considerably limited resources when competing with formidable opponents. A week after the conclusion of the America's Cup, I got a puppy and named it Kiwi (Kiwi Magic was an under*dog*, after all). When I was starting my software company, I needed a code name for the project. I was so happy with the puppy that I called the project Kiwi. Eventually, the day to file documents of incorporation came, and no better name had been found than Kiwi. So it stuck. What better paradigm for a startup software company facing behemoths such as Microsoft and Aldus?"

Kurta

The word kurta means "message" in ancient Sanskrit. Likewise, the Phoenix-based manufacturer of graphics tablets views its products as useful for sending messages to computers.

MACROMIND

MacroMind

After originally founding their Illinois-based company as Chicago Software in April of 1984, Marc Canter and Jay Fenton realized they wanted a name that would better reflect their flamboyance. So three days after its birth, Chicago Software transmogrified into MacroMind, a name taken from an evil creature that Fenton had created for an unreleased Bally coin-op video game. The company has since merged with Paracomp and Authorware, and now goes by the name Macromedia.

MicroMat

Founded in February of 1989 to market MicroRx, a repair guide for Mac trouble-shooting, MicroMat was actually named by a Mac. Founder Jeff Baudin explains: "We were really stuck for a company name. Everything we thought up was awful. Finally, I decided to write a Hyper-Card stack to help me. I threw together a simple little thing called Namer. It had three columns: two of the columns contained name portions, the third would be where these portions were randomly put together. MicroMat is actually an amalgamation of Microsoft and PhotoMat. I still use the stack to this day. That's how we came up with the name DriveTech for our floppy diagnostic program. In fact, looking at a list of some old product name runs I had done, I discovered a number of suggestions that have since been used by other companies, including PowerBook and Quadra!"

Microsoft®

Microsoft

Born in the summer of 1975 in Albuquerque, New Mexico, Microsoft is an abbreviation of microcomputer software. The company was originally called Micro-Soft, but soon the hyphen was dropped and, in a departure from the industry fascination with intercaps, the capital letter S was changed to lowercase.

Mysterium Tremendum

When you develop entertainment and educational software (such as Global Trespass, Moriarty's Revenge, and Moriarty's Return), you had better be creative all the way down to your name. Would you trust the American Software Company to develop the next great, imaginative game? Such was the thinking that led James Harvey to choose the name Mysterium Tremendum for his firm. The name comes from Rudolf Otto, an early 20th century German philosopher/theologian, who in *The Idea of the Holy*, used the term to describe the presence of God. As he says, it is a feeling that "arouses spasms and convulsions...erupts into strange excitement...ecstasy...or in its wild demonic form, grizzly horror and shuddering." In other words, it is an inexpressible mystery that leaves one trembling. "When I sit in front of my 'tabula rasa' computer screen ready to create a new game," explains Harvey, "I feel a bit like a god and hope I can create software which gives others a taste of the Mysterium Tremendum."

O P C O D E
S Y S T E M S   I N C

3950 Fabian Way • Palo Alto, CA 94303
(4 1 5)   8 5 6 - 3 3 3 3

Opcode Systems Inc.

Opcode was originally created to develop and publish
the programming code of founder, Dave Oppenheim.
Ergo, Opcode.

PASSPORT®

Passport Designs

Dave Kusek, president and founder, had come up with
a long list of potential names for his music software company. Of the candidates, Passport Designs, was eventually
chosen because of its universal association with the idea
of travel and the desire to convey the image that the
firm's products would, psychologically and intellectually,
take the user to another place.

R A Y   D R E A M

Ray Dream, Inc.

Sorry to break it to you, but contrary to popular belief,
there is no Mr. Raymond Dream. The company's flagship
product, Ray Dream Designer, was code-named Mind
Tracer and had a logo showing some brains spewing out
of a crane. According to president Eric Hautemont, "Both

205

the name and logo were deemed too ugly, so we went looking for something else. Since the company's core technology was a computer graphics algorithm known as ray tracing, we decided on Ray Dream. We liked it because it was a word play on 'ray tracing' and 'day dream,' as well as a dig at Pixar's famous *Red's Dream* computer-generated cartoon."

In addition to Ray Dream Designer, the company also publishes JAG, a nifty anti-aliasing utility. Ray Dream originally wanted to call the product JEDI (Jagged Edges Disappear Immediately) but couldn't come to an agreement with the LucasFilm legal department. That's when David Biedny, of Industrial Light & Magic fame, sprang to the rescue by suggesting the acronym which stands for Jaggies Are Gone.

radius™

Radius

Founders Mike Boich (the first Apple evangelist), Burrell Smith (the original Mac hardware designer), Matt Carter (manager of the Mac factory), and Alain Rossman were looking for a name under which to market their full page display back in May of 1986. They liked the sound of *radius*, the fact that it is easy to both spell and pronounce, and over the long haul, a mathematical term is less likely to become dated than a technical term.

RASTEROPS

RasterOps

Founded in 1987 by Keith Sorenson, this display system manufacturer gets its name from the term "raster operations". *In Principals of Interactive Computer Graphics*, author Newman Sproull defines the term as an order in which raster values are altered, or simply stated, the way in which lines are arranged on the monitor to create an image.

Sentient Software

While working at Apple on April Fools' Day in 1988, David Shayer wrote an extension that powered down a Mac II soon after it was turned on. After inflicting his practical joke on his co-workers, he realized they would certainly seek revenge, so he whipped up a little program to lock his hard disk. The program was so successful in preventing his victims from planting their own little surprises on his Mac that they simply stole all of his memory. During the next six months, Shayer spent nights and weekends fleshing out the program until it was so solid that over 100 people inside Apple were personally using it on their Macs. Ultimately Fifth Generation Systems agreed to acquire the program, now called DiskLock, and Shayer quit Apple in 1990 to start his own development company, Sentient Software. Shayer admits that "the name Sentient Software is kind of an inside joke. Sentient of course means self aware, conscious, or feeling, and is a reference to artificial intelligence (AI). But of course there is no real AI nowadays, and probably won't be for 50 years or more, and we don't even work on that type of software. But I'm fascinated by AI—real artificial intelligence—not the expert systems in use today."

Shiva

Shiva

In Hinduism, Shiva represents "the destroyer," the third deity of the Trimurti, but that is not what co-founders Frank Slaughter and Dan Schwinn had in mind when they named their networking products company. One day, while reading a magazine, Slaughter came upon an article about the world's most powerful laser fusion project which was in progress at Lawrence Livermore Labs. Its code name was Shiva. They simply liked the sound of Shiva and adopted it as the name of their company.

SILICON BEACH
S O F T W A R E

Silicon Beach Software

Founder Charlie Jackson was considering calling his software company I-5 Software in honor of the interstate highway that runs from his San Diego headquarters to San Francisco's Silicon Valley. But thinking better of the idea, Jackson settled instead on the nickname—Silicon

Beach—that some locals in the computer circles had given to San Diego. Jackson admits he sometimes got letters addressed to *Silicone* Beach, but that's a different place entirely. Silicon Beach Software was eventually acquired by Aldus and became its consumer division.

Silicon Valley Bus Company

As Avery Dee and friends gathered around a fireplace in December, 1990 to think of a name for his new company that would specialize in hardware peripherals for the Apple Desktop Bus (that's where keyboards and mice connect to the Mac), they were convinced that the world didn't need another Exceltronics, Technostratopheric Systems, or the like. They wanted something a little whimsical, a bit irreverent, but also meaningful. One of those assembled said, "Avery, you've been a bus rider (meaning doing hardware that plugs into buses) for almost 15 years, why don't you call it The Bus Company?" Recalls Dee, "We all knew it was instantly great! Silicon Valley was added to impart some geographic identity and further imply that we had something to do with electronic stuff." And thus, dear reader, Silicon Valley Bus Company was founded in January 1991 in Los Gatos, California and has enjoyed success with products such as BC-91 (a bar code reader) and MultiPort (a six port, software-controlled serial switch).

Sir-Tech Software

This entertainment software publisher, famous for its Wizardy line of adventure games, was originally called Sir-O-Tech, a derivative of the surname of co-founder and CEO, Fred Sirotek. Sirotek is an uncommon Czech name which, when loosely translated, means "those who stand alone."

Software Toolworks

The founders wanted to convey the idea of their software as useful products, or tools that could be used by the average person without intimidation. "Works" was added to provide the image of the place where an artisan—such as a blacksmith—creates an item of fine craftsmanship. Thus when customers hear the name Software Toolworks, they are supposed to imagine a place where quality software tools are created.

STF Technologies

Many people think that the name of this company must stand for the founders' initials, but nothing could be further from the truth. Founders Doug Troxell and Jim Wilcox were working on a fax modem project for a public telephone company when, prompted by regulatory changes and the entrepreneurial spirit, they decided to start their own company. In keeping with the theme of communications products for the Mac, they decided to call the firm Semaphore Corporation and dubbed their product JTFax, for Just The Fax. All was well until the lawyers informed them that the name was already taken. In a moment of despair someone jokingly suggested they use a line—Fax Signals To Follow—from a promotional item as the new name. Figuring it was so bizarre that no one could have used it before, the name of their fax modem was shortened to Fax^{STF} and the company assumed the moniker STF Technologies.

STRATA

Strata

Strata, a leader in computer-assisted visualization tools for designers and illustrators, was founded in St. George, Utah in April of 1988 by two brothers: Gary and Ken Bringhurst. Both had been students at Brigham Young

211

University, where they discussed the idea of developing a powerful three-dimensional illustration program. One day they were discussing what they should call their product and the company that would produce it. While brainstorming, Ken looked up and gazed upon one of St. George's beautiful red rock mountains. Since another one of his brothers was a geologist, his attention was drawn to the layers or the "stratum" of the rock. Equating the layers of the rock to the layers of the software program they were developing, the brothers decided to call the company Strata.

SYNEX

SYNEX

President Allen Lubow is a long-time advocate of the work of Buckminster Fuller, the novelist who coined the word "synergy," which means the whole is more than the sum of its parts. This struck a chord with Lubow, who was looking for a short, corporate sounding name for his new software company. "Someone had told me the story of the name Kodak; three hard consonants, two vowels, and no meaning at all. So I chose SYNEX. Except for the problem of people pronouncing it with a long I as in Sinex (the cold relief medicine), it has worked very well." SYNEX is pronounced "sin x," by the way.

Teknosys inc.

Teknosys

Although it's best known now for its Help! series of intelligent system diagnostic utilities, Tampa-based Teknosys was founded in September 1988 to sell a compiler for HyperCard XCMD programmers called HyperBASIC. "The name Teknosys comes from three root words: TEchnology, KNOwledge and SYStems," explains president Steve Smoot. "When we were originally thinking of a name, these were the key concepts. We spent a lot of time trying to think of names. We tried name-generating software, word associations, etc. It wasn't until I was talking to my wife, Kim, that we actually came up with a name. She had the idea while we were sitting in a restaurant, resting at Disney World. Four months after we came up with the name, another company created a name that was pronounced the same but spelled differently, TechGnosis. What do you think the chances are that two companies that produced Mac software and were based in Florida would choose the same name?"

Thunderware

Thunderware

In early 1974, Vic Bull and Tom Petrie decided to form a consulting group and wanted a company name that was distinct and reflected the goals of the new company: to design and develop integrated hardware, software, and firmware solutions. They felt that the company name should have impact, much like a "clap of thunder." The logical choice, ThunderClap, sounded too off-beat, so the two founders settled on the name Thunderware.

Timeworks

Although it has gained recognition in the Mac marketplace with its curiously-named Publish It! (say it really fast and you'll know what I mean) line of DTP applications, Timeworks began in 1982 as a developer of software for the Timex Sinclair 1000. The founders had already constructed mock-up packages using the company name Softworks only to discover that a small Chicago publisher owned the rights to that name. As vice president Vic Schiller tells the story, "We wanted to use the packages as they were laid out, so we needed four new letters." Vic's wife came up with the name Timeworks, and since it looked good on the box, the name stuck.

T/Maker®

T/Maker

Although best known for ClickArt and WriteNow, the T/Maker name comes from the company's original 1979 product, a program for calculating rows and columns of numbers. The program was originally called "the table maker," but that was too long, so the name was shortened to T/Maker. "We hadn't even heard of an 'electronic spreadsheet' until VisiCalc came out six months later," adds president Heidi Roizen.

The Official History of the Dogcow

Have you ever wondered about that strange animal depicted in the Page Setup dialog box for some Apple printers, such as the LaserWriter?

Courtesy of Apple Computer, Inc.

The dogcow in the LaserWriter Page Setup Options dialog box.

That's the mysterious dogcow, which was the subject of an equally mysterious Technical Note that Apple distributed to developers in an otherwise serious batch of information sent out in April of 1989. The Apple-sanctioned Tech Note #31 appeared in print only this once, but the dogcow lives on to this day. What started as an April Fools' prank has spawned a worldwide cult of Clarus.

I approached Mark Harlan, the author of Tech Note #31, about the possibility of reproducing it in this book. That wasn't possible, but he was gracious enough to grant me permission to reprint the following "History of the Dogcow" that originally appeared as a two-part story in *develop*, The Apple Technical Journal. Enjoy!

How It All Began

The dogcow was originally a character in the Cairo font that used to ship with the Macintosh; it was designed by Susan Kare. I had always been interested in this critter ever since I first saw it in the LaserWriter Page Setup Options dialog, sometime during my stint in Apple's Developer Technical Support (DTS) group in 1987. To me it showed perfection in human interface design. With one picture it was very easy to explain concepts like an inverted image or larger print area that otherwise would be nearly impossible to communicate.

Interest became an obsession when one day I was talking to Scott ("Zz") Zimmerman about the dialog and suddenly thought, "Just what is that animal supposed to be, anyway?" Since Zz was the Printing Guy in DTS (now in the Newton group), and my favorite pastime was to bother him endlessly anyway, I started pressing him on whether the animal was a dog or a cow.

In an act of desperation he said, "It's both, OK? It's called a 'dogcow.' Now will you get out of my office?" The date was October 15, 1987, and I consider this to be the first use of the term. It should be noted that since then a few people (including Ginger herself) have told me that actually the phrase was coined by Ginger Jernigan (ex-DTS, now ROM software) at a meeting of Apple's Print Shop sometime shortly before that, which very well could be the case. Nevertheless it was Zz who pressed it into common usage, and he certainly was the first person I ever heard use the term.

Zz's ploy to get me out of his office was futile, however, because then I stood around and postulated that the dogcow's

217

genes would have a radical effect on its behavior, and it must not bark or moo, but rather utter a combination like "Boo-woo!" or "Moof!" We both thought it was funny enough that we decided to press it into everyday usage, and I started circulating the dogcow with "Moof!" on internal memos. The idea caught on, and at the 1988 Worldwide Developers Conference we gave away dogcow buttons in the debugging lab. Louella Pizzuti (ex-DTS, ex-*develop* editor, now citizen of the world) came up with the great idea of making the background Mountain Dew green. Response to the buttons was huge, and no one was smiling more than the DTS folks when John Sculley wore one for his keynote speech. It was a major-league coup.

The Origin of Tech Note #31

Then things started to spin out of control. Various groups internally started picking up the dogcow logo and doing things that didn't seem, well, DTS-like. The final straw was when the dogcow pin appeared in a Microsoft advertisement. Mark Johnson (ex-DTS, now in Apple Europe) approached me and suggested that we throw down the gauntlet and write a Technical Note on the subject. I balked out of nothing more than sheer laziness.

Some time passed and we were getting ready to go with the April 1989 batch of Tech Notes when Mark approached me again, saying that he thought having an April Fools' edition describing the dogcow would be perfect. I said yes but then stalled and stalled, missing two deadlines, and I thought the Tech Note wasn't going to happen. Mark marched in my office one day in March of 1989 at 11:30 A.M. announcing that Tech Notes were shipping at noon and implied that my manliness was in question if I

didn't get that Note in the batch. My macho instincts just couldn't allow that to happen, so Tech Note #31, "The Dogcow," was written in literally 40 minutes in one pass. I'd been thinking about it for quite some time, so I knew pretty much how it would go; I just sat down and typed it out. Given more time I definitely would have churned out something a bit more polished, and part of its quirkiness, I'm sure, is due to the time pressure I was under.

One thing was certain: it had to be something original in concept. I've always had a deep disdain for people who rip off comedic stuff. You know, the same people who used to have to tell all their jokes with an English accent because of Monty Python are now those who say "Not!" behind phrases. Once is funny, but after a while it gets really old. I definitely wanted it out of the mainstream.

For numbering I wanted to use the letter e, but Mark pointed out that there had been confusion early on in the Tech Note numbering scheme and that a few numbers had been left out for various reasons. He showed me some conversations from the net that went on and on about Tech Note #31 and people's guesses as to why it was missing. (People were really, really out there with their guessing; anyone who's a believer in conspiracy theories would have enjoyed this blatant gibberish.) The number 31 had the right feel; it would blend into the regular batch better than the letter e, and I've always had a soft spot for prime numbers, so we picked it.

Sports Illustrated had run a great fake story about a Zen baseball pitcher sometime earlier and we borrowed their idea of having the words "April Fools'" spelled out within the article—in our case using the first letter of every line of the poem at the closing. No one has ever mentioned this to me, so few people must have caught it.

There's a picture of the wrong way to draw the dogcow that several people thought was a scanned image of Zz. Actually, completely independently of the Tech Note, I'd been using a program called Mac-a-Mug, designed to make mug shots, and came across a set of hair that looked frighteningly like Zz's. After fiddling around with the program a bit I was able to come up with a good rendition of Zz's head, and I shoved it into the Tech Note without his ever knowing about it. The expression (and color) of his face when he learned about the picture is a memory I'll always cherish.

The Note also contains the expression "Aanal, Enacku Naiimadu, Kaanali!" People came up with very unusual anagrams or unusual explanations for what it meant, the best being that it was an obscure reference to a clip of *The Day the Earth Stood Still* that had been cut from the film. But the truth is that it's phoneticized Tamil that was supplied by Sriram Subramanian (Networking Guy, ex-DTS, ex-Taligent, now in Apple Japan) meaning "But I can't see the dogcow!"

Ironically, there's also a mistake in that the "correct" way to draw the dogcow is actually wrong. We ended up being so pressured for time in getting the Note out the door that we just jammed it into a weird PostScript file that ended up mutating the shape. Shortly after the release of that Note, Chris Derossi (ex-DTS, now at General Magic) convinced me that a better solution was to have the correct way to draw the dogcow be pixelated, to avoid these idiosyncrasies in the future—which is what's now done.

Distribution of Tech Note #31

Mark Johnson and I both thought that since Tech Note #31 was an April Fools' joke anyway, the best thing would be to just include it in the April monthly mailing to Apple Partners and Associates; we'd drop it from the subsequent batches, with the direct intent of making it a curio. The idea was that the people who were currently in the Macintosh community would get it and everyone else wouldn't. We very intentionally were trying to build an aura around it. The April 1989 mailing is the only time this Tech Note was ever in print under the official auspices of Apple.

There was a bit of a lag time between the writing of the Note and the actual release; by the time it went out, I actually had forgotten about it. The response was immediate and intense. Internally I received a couple of vaguely threatening calls from people claiming false ownership, but the overwhelming majority of people thought it was great. One gentleman in the developer community took offense saying that "dogcow" was too close to "Dachau" and showed how the note had underpinnings of anti-Semitism. (I showed this one to my Jewish father-in-law, who had to be resuscitated, he was laughing so hard.)

Aside from that, it really struck a chord with the developer community like nothing I've seen before or since. I received about 40 pieces of fan mail that month. Developer Technical Support (DTS) must have gone for a year before there was a batch of e-mail that didn't have a dogcow reference in it. In fact, to this day people say to me, "Mark Harlan? I know your name from Tech Notes"—but it's the only one I ever wrote.

221

Then came the concept of a Developer CD as a vehicle for distributing Tech Notes electronically (along with sample code and more). I was overseeing that project, and immediately we had an interesting conundrum: We wanted all information in electronic format, yet what were we going to do with Tech Note #31? Merely slipping it into the Tech Notes stack seemed like disaster, but then it didn't really feel right to omit it.

Again, it was Mark Johnson who came to the rescue with the excellent idea of burying the Tech Note. So on the early CD, "Phil and Dave's Excellent CD," you have to go through a bizarre sequence of commands to bring it up. Even now, tradition requires that I not give the details, but it involves Shift-Option-clicking and typing "grazing off a cliff," and it emits "Moof!" and "Foom!" sounds. (For the "Moof!" sound we took a real cow and then Zz said "fff" into a MacRecorder; the "Foom!" is just the same sound played backwards.) It took a while for anyone to find the Note using any technique, and I've never heard of anyone doing it except through ResEdit.

The Note stayed on the first few Developer CDs. The access technique changed from disc to disc, and not even I knew how to do it after the original "Phil and Dave." Somewhere along the line the Note was dropped from the CD altogether.

Other Dogcow Paraphernalia

Bootleg T-shirts started appearing. There was an apartment near Apple headquarters that started flying a dogcow flag. The stack version of the Note had a watermarked background that someone removed pixel by pixel before posting it to the Internet. Several developers were nearly

thrown out of a movie theater at MacHack for "Moofing" before a movie.

In addition to the Tech Note there are three pins: green background, the most common; red background with Kanji (the word on the pin actually is pronounced "Moo-aann!" because Japanese dogs don't woof, they say something like "aann-aann"); and the super-rare red background with "Moof!," which are misprints of the Kanji batch. Also, there's a dogcow window sticker. All of these were given away in DTS labs, and all but the window sticker have been collected up a long time ago.

If you think of the dogcow fathers as being Zz Zimmerman, Mark Johnson, and me, there's only one dogcow shirt that received our supervision and approval: the black DTS sweatshirt with the small dogcow on the chest (designed by Toni Trujillo). I also designed the graphic for a DTS gift that was a shoulder bag with all incarnations of the dogcow on it (flipped, rotated, and inverted). Unfortunately the bag was incredibly cheap and most of them have self-destructed.

Chris Derossi and Mary Burke designed a dogcow mousepad and even went so far as to call Pepsi-Cola to get the exact color of Mountain Dew green for the background. They made 500 of these and I wrote an insert that went into the packaging. Aside from the original Tech Note, it's the only thing I've ever written about dogcattle—excluding this story.

Dogcow Trivia

Somewhere along the line I baptized the dogcow "Clarus." Of course she's a female, as are all cows; males would be referred to as dogbulls, but none exist because there are already bulldogs, and God doesn't like to have naming problems.

Now things are much bigger than they were then—both in number of developers and number of Apple employees. The dogcow regularly appears on documents that are no longer connected to DTS, or in some cases (such as Scott Knaster's books) not even from Apple. In a sense, the dogcow has become mainstream; people are copying it—and that's exactly what I was fighting against in the first place (not to mention that she, and her "Moof!" cry, are bona fide trademarks of Apple Computer). To put a stop to all this, I'm threatening to kill her off, but the editor of *develop* has become such a fan that she's not sure she'll accept a "Dogcow is Dead" column. Stay tuned!

Steve Jobs wanted to avoid licensing copyrighted typefaces—such as Times, Century, Helvetica, and Gothic—for the Mac, so he instructed artist Susan Kare to design knockoffs. Kare, who had grown up in the suburbs of Philadelphia, wanted to name her fonts after the railroad stations of the Paoli Local train: Ardmore, Merion, Rosmont, etc. Jobs liked the idea of using city names, but instisted on world-class cities that corresponded to the original typefaces: New York (Times), Geneva Helvetica), London (Old English), etc. The frivolous font known as San Francisco was originally named Ransom, because documents created with it looked like kidnappers' notes. By the way, Kare designed all the original Mac fonts except Venice, which was the creation of Bill Atkinson.

About the Author

Courtesy of Apple Computer, Inc.

Mark "The Red" Harlan, author of Tech Note #31.

Mark Harlan started life in Rawlins, Wyoming, and has led about exactly the kind of life you'd expect as a result. He spent most of his six years at Apple finding employees who were hired by Steve Jobs and asking them, "So how does it feel knowing that the way you changed the world is by putting Windows on all PCs?" After leaving Apple, he went through extensive deprogramming. Unfortunately, the therapy didn't hold and he has since joined yet another cult: General Magic. In a recent interview, Mark was asked if he had any words of wisdom on the dogcow. "Yeah. Warn everyone that both the dogcow logo and 'Moof!' are trademarks of Apple Computer. You don't ever want to be in the position of having to answer 'What are you in for?' with 'Bootleg T-shirts.'"

About *develop*

"The History of the Dogcow" is from *develop*, The Apple Technical Journal, Issues 17 and 18, and is reprinted here with permission of Apple Computer, Inc. *develop*, Apple's award-winning quarterly technical journal, provides an in-depth look at code and techniques that have been reviewed for robustness by Apple engineers. Each issue comes with a CD that contains the source code for that issue, as well as all back issues, Technical Notes, sample code, and other useful software and documentation. Subscriptions to *develop* are available through APDA (1-800-282-2732), AppleLink: Dev.Subs, or Internet: Dev.Subs@AppleLink.Apple.com.

Easter Egg Hunt

For the most part, the programmers and engineers at Apple are an extremely talented bunch with a good sense of humor. Unfortunately, they must often spend countless hours working on rather mundane projects that bring them precious little fame and glory. One way they strike back at "the establishment" is by hiding secret messages in their creations. These messages are intentionally difficult to find (perhaps so that they can sneak by non-technical supervisors?). To activate them, you must usually perform the digital equivalent of standing on your head and asking "Mother, may I?" Since you must hunt for them, these secret messages are affectionately known as Easter eggs.

Whenever Apple releases a new piece of System software, scores of dedicated Easter egg hunters immediately tear open the files with ResEdit looking for clues in the resources. Then they "thrash" the programs, clicking everywhere in sight while holding down every imaginable key combination looking for the elusive trigger. At the risk of spoiling such fun, here are the precise instructions for uncovering some of the most interesting Easter eggs ever hidden by Apple employees.

AppleFax Modem

While holding down the button on the front, turn on the modem. The modem beeps three times. After the three beeps, press the button three times in the same rhythm as the beeps. If your timing is right, the modem pronounces the names of the three Apple engineers who worked on the modem (Peter, Alan, and Neal).

Cache Switch

Open the Cache Switch control panel, click Option, then click the version number. The 040 icon slides over, revealing the name of the programmer.

Choose Show Balloons from the Balloon Help menu and move the cursor over the version number. The balloon reads "Wink, Wink!"

Caps Lock

Choose Show Balloons from the Balloon Help menu and move the cursor over the Caps Lock file icon in the Finder. Alternatively, install the Caps Lock extension, turn on Balloon Help, press the Caps Lock key, and move the cursor over the up-arrow icon in the menu bar. The balloon reads: "This file allows your Macintosh TIM or Derringer to display an icon in the menu bar to indicate that caps lock is on." TIM and Derringer were the code names of the first PowerBooks.

Somebody apparently forgot to remove the code name references from the extension released with System 7.0.1. Subsequent versions do not have this Easter egg.

Color

Open the Color control panel under System 7 and click the sample text, holding down the mouse button. The words "sample text" are replaced with "by Dean Yu" and if you click and hold again, the words "& Vincent Lo" appear. These are the two Apple programmers responsible for the control panel.

Disk Archive/Retrieval Tool

Holding down the Option key, choose About DART from the File menu. In addition to the normal information on version numbers and copyright dates, the window displays the name of the programmer, David Mutter, and those he wishes to thank.

FaxMaker

Choose About FaxMaker from the Apple menu, then click the icon. The arrow pointer changes into a mouse, and a scrolling list of the developers appears.

Installer

Double-click Installer 3.0.1 (the version that comes with System 6.0.7 and 6.0.8), and click OK, then type "ski" to present an alert box in which you can choose from five wait-cursors: hand with counting fingers, spinning globe, spinning disc, wristwatch, and dots that move. The custom cursor only works while the Installer is running; it doesn't become the System-wide wait cursor.

Double-click Installer 3.2 (the version that comes with System 7), and click OK, then hold down Command-Option. The Help button becomes the About button. Click it to see the names of the programmers, beta testers, and friends.

Labels

Open the Labels control panel under System 7 and delete all of the label names by repeatedly pressing tab, then delete. When all of the names are blank, close the control panel and choose Restart from the Finder's Special menu. Now if you pull down the Labels menu in the Finder, the first item is still None, but the remaining seven labels spell out "ALANJEF," the names of the Apple programmers who wrote this control panel.

Macintosh Classic

Hold down Command-Option-X-O (the Classic's code name was XO) and turn on the computer to start up running System 6.0.3, Finder 6.1x, and AppleShare from a ROM-disk. This secret disk is contained in the read-only memory of the Classic and may not be altered.

Apparently the ROM-disk was supposed to allow the Classic to be sold as a diskless workstation, but Apple abandoned that marketing angle without removing the capability from the machine.

Using a program able to see invisible files (like ResEdit, Norton Utilities, or MacTools), examine the ROM-disk for a "Brought to you by" folder containing more hidden folders bearing the names of the Classic designers.

Macintosh IIci

Open the General Controls control panel and set the date to 9/20/89 (the release date of the Mac IIci). Choose Restart from the Finder's Special menu, then immediately hold down Command-Option-C-I. In a few seconds,

a color picture of the IIci design team appears. Click the mouse to continue.

Macintosh IIfx

Open the General Controls control panel and set the date to 3/19/90 (the release date of the IIfx). Choose Restart from the Finder's Special menu, then immediately hold down Command-Option-F-X. In a few seconds, a color picture of the IIfx design team appears. Click the mouse to continue.

Macintosh Plus

Inside the Mac Plus there are two switches accessible only if an optional pair of buttons called the programmer's switch is installed toward the rear on the left side. In the Finder, with no other applications open, press the rear part of the programmer's switch to generate an interrupt. A blank window appears. This is the Mac's built-in debugger used by knowledgeable programmers. Enter "G 40E118" (that's a zero, not the letter O), then press Return to see a tiny "Stolen from Apple Computer" message in the upper left-hand corner of your screen. To exit the debugger, press the front part of the programmer's switch to reset the Mac.

Apparently the "Stolen from..." message is a form of copyright protection so that Apple can easily determine if a clone manufacturer has simply copied its read-only memory.

Macintosh SE

Press the rear part of the programmer's switch to generate an interrupt. The blank debugger window appears. Enter "G 41D89A" and press Return. Four pictures of the Mac SE development team appear as a slideshow. To exit the debugger, press the front part of the programmer's switch to reset the Mac. The engineers were able to include these digitized pictures because they based the Mac SE on the same 256-kilobyte ROMs in the Mac II, but the Mac SE didn't need many of the things contained therein, so there was plenty of extra space in which to hide their Easter egg.

 Also, try entering "G 4188A4" into the debugger. This presents a "Stolen from Apple Computer" message in the upper left-hand corner of your screen.

Macintosh SE/30

Press the rear part of the programmer's switch to generate an interrupt. The blank debugger window appears. Enter "DM 4082E853 20" and press Return to display a few bytes of memory from location 4082E853 onwards. The bytes there spell out, in ASCII, "WHAT ARE YOU STARING AT?" Also, try entering "G 04D98A" into the debugger.

MacPaint 2.0

Hold down Tab-Space while choosing About MacPaint from the Apple menu to display a painting of a nude zebra-striped woman atop a white zebra. The painting is by well-known erotic artist Olivia de Berardinis. When

Claris discovered this Easter egg, it was quickly removed, so only very early copies contain this image.

MacsBug

Choose Show Balloons from the Balloon Help menu, then move the cursor over the MacsBug file icon in the Finder. The balloon reads "This file provides programmers with information proving that it really was a hardware problem."

Map

Open the Map control panel, enter "MID" as the city name, then click Find. The map centers on a flashing point in the south Atlantic which represents the "Middle of Nowhere."

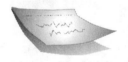

Clicking on the map version number inserts both the version number and "by Mark Davis" (the programmer) into the city name field until you release the mouse button.

Memory

Open the Memory control panel under System 7. Turn on Virtual Memory and hold down Option while clicking on the Select Hard Disk pop-up menu to present the first names of the programmers; each name has a submenu with a few comments.

Monitors

Open the Monitors control panel under System 7, then click the version number to see a short list of the programmers. While you hold down the mouse button, tap

Option several times and the little smiley face sticks out
its tongue. After repeatedly tapping Option, the names
are rearranged and some first and last names get replaced
with "Blue" or "Meanies," a reference to the nickname of
the System 7 quality-control team.

MultiFinder 1.0

Hold down Command-Option while choosing About
MultiFinder from the Apple menu to display a scrolling
list of credits.

MultiFinder 6.0

Choose About MultiFinder from the Apple menu and
leave the alert box on screen for about an hour or more.
Eventually you see the message "I want my l—k and f—l"
(that's "look and feel," in case you were wondering).

PowerBook

Open the PowerBook control panel and Option-click
the version number to display a credits dialog box.

QuickTime

Choose Show Balloons from the Balloon Help menu,
then move the cursor over the QuickTime extension file.
The balloon reads "Time n. A nonspatial continuum in
which events occur in apparently irreversible succession
from the past to the present to the future."

ResEdit

Hold down Shift-Option-Command as you choose About
ResEdit from the Apple menu. You get the chance to enter
"pig mode" (oink oink oink). When you put ResEdit into
pig mode, resources are compacted and purged each time

ResEdit goes through its event loop (several times a second). Since this makes ResEdit slower, it's not of much use, except that you get to hear the funny pig noises.

Also, just try holding down only Command-Option while choosing About ResEdit from the Apple menu to display credits.

Simple Player

Hold down Option as you choose About Simple Player from the Apple menu. The two movie frames now have gray-scale cats in them.

System 6.0.7J

Open the General Controls control panel and set the date to 1/1/92, then choose Restart from the Finder's Special menu. The startup screen displays "Happy New Year" in Japanese. This only works with the KanjiTalk version of the System software.

System 7

Insert an unlocked floppy disk into a drive and click on its name in the Finder. Change the name to either "KMEG JJ KS" or "Hello world JS N A DTP" (enter exactly as shown without the quotation marks, paying attention to upper- and lower-case letters). Press Command-E to eject the disk. Click the dimmed disk icon that remains on the desktop to present an alert box that asks you to "Please insert the disk: HFS for 7.0 by dnf and ksct." These are the initials of David N. Feldman and Kenny S. C. Tung, the two Apple engineers responsible for updating the hierarchical filing system.

System 7

Press Option and look in the Apple menu. The first item, About This Macintosh, changes to About The Finder. Choose it to see a picture of mountains which first appeared in System 1.0.

If the creation date of the invisible Desktop Folder is May 13, 1991 (the release date of System 7), or later, wait a few seconds and the names of all the Finder developers through Mac and Lisa history scroll by along the bottom of the window.

 If you press Command-Option while choosing About The Finder, the arrow cursor turns into a goofy face.

System File

Open the System file with a word processor (you may have to choose an option such as "Open All File Types") to see a frivolous distress call from the development team. If you are using System 6, the message is "Help! Help! We're being held prisoner in a system software factory!" Under System 7, the message is "Help! Help! We're still being held prisoner in a system software factory!" The message is followed by the names of the Blue Meanies, Apple's System 7 quality-control team. After viewing this Easter egg, just close the document; don't try saving the file or you may seriously screw up your Mac.

TeachText

 In TeachText, press Option and choose About TeachText from the Apple menu to display the standard credits alert box expanded to include the names of people the programmers wish to thank.

The Hunt Continues

The Easter eggs listed here are limited to Apple products, but there are hundreds of Easter eggs hidden in third-party products, and I can't find them all myself. If you know of any other interesting Easter eggs, please send me detailed instructions on how to activate them and I'll add them to my growing list.

Owen W. Linzmayer

2227 15th Avenue

San Francisco, CA 94116-1824

AppleLink: Owen

America Online: Owen Ink

CompuServe: 71333,3152

Taking Trademarks to the Bank

Want to get rich? It's easy. Just think up a whole bunch of cool product names and create a few nifty logos, then secure the trademarks and sit tight. If you're lucky, eventually Apple will decide it just has to have the rights to your trademark. Now you're in the position to ask for whatever you think Apple will pay. If these following cases are any example, the sky's the limit, so think big and carry a hot-shot lawyer in your hip pocket.

Apple Battles Beatles

When Steve Jobs first proposed Apple Computer as a name for the company he would found with Steve Wozniak in 1976, it briefly occurred to Woz that they might have some trouble with Apple Corps, the Beatles' recording company, but he dismissed the thought. Perhaps they should have done a little more brainstorming, because that name would end up costing them dearly.

As it turned out, Woz was right; Apple Corps didn't take kindly to anyone infringing on their trademark, and in November 1981, Apple Computer and Apple Corps entered into a secret agreement that placed certain restrictions on the use and registration of their respective "Apple" trademarks. Essentially, Apple Computer paid the British company an undisclosed sum for the worldwide rights to use the "Apple" name on computer products, but Apple Corps retained the rights in the music field.

In February 1989, Apple Corps filed suit against Apple Computer in London seeking unspecified damages, charging that Apple violated the terms of the trademark coexistence agreement by marketing products with music synthesizing capabilities. Specifically cited in the suit were the Mac Plus, SE, and II; the Apple IIGS and IIGS upgrade kit for the Apple IIe; the Apple CD SC drive; and Apple's MIDI (Musical Instrument Digital Interface) device. The Beatles' law firm suggested that Apple change its name to Banana or Peach if it wanted to continue making music products, and estimated that Apple Corps would ultimately be paid $50 million to $200 million in royalties. Although Apple maintained that it had not broken the 1981 agreement, on October 9, 1991, it settled the suit by paying Apple Corps $26.5 million.

When Apple Corps sued Apple in 1989, System 7 was still under development. One of the new features of System 7 was the ability to record your own system beeps in the Sound control panel using a microphone. An astute engineer realized that Apple Corps might take umbrage at the Mac's ability to record voice and music. In an act of defiance, the engineer created a new system beep called Sosumi (pronounced "so sue me").

Cold Cash for Classic

As it prepared to make a serious push into the low-end of the market with its October 1990 introduction of three new computers—the Mac Classic, LC, and IIsi—Apple got some unwelcome news. Someone else already owned the computer-industry trademark rights to the "Classic" name: Modular Computer Systems Inc. of Fort Lauderdale, Florida, manufacturer of the ModComp Classic, a series of real-time computer systems for the control and automation markets. Apparently Apple was very much enamored of the "Classic" name because it entered into a five-year, renewable $1 million contract to acquire the rights to the name for use in the personal computer market.

What's the Big Idea?

In 1991, Alfred J. Mandel founded a Palo Alto-based marketing consulting firm called the Big Idea Group (BIG) and produced a calligraphic logo of a light bulb, the universal cartoon symbol for an idea. Soon after Apple began promoting its Newton technology, Mandel received calls from friends asking if he had had anything to do with the personal digital assistant because the Newton logo Apple was using in its brochures and advertisements looked suspiciously like the BIG logo.

SEPARATED AT BIRTH?

BIG IDEA GROUP   NEWTON

Mandel initially offered Apple a non-exclusive license to use his firm's logo on the Newton. After all, he had worked at Apple from 1982 to 1986—first on printer products for the Lisa and then as the event marketing manager for the Macintosh—and he bore no ill will toward his former employer. Uncomfortable with such an arrangement, Apple's legal department tried to establish that the BIG logo was based upon prior art. Anxious to avoid a protracted lawsuit, Mandel sold Apple the logo on July 29, 1993, with the provision that he could continue using it for one year. Terms of the settlement remain confidential to this day.

Cosmos Carl

The November 29, 1993 issue of *MacWEEK* featured a cover story on three computers Apple would introduce on March 14, 1994, as the Power Macintosh 6100/60, 7100/66, and 8100/80. The story mentioned in passing that the computers went by the code names PDM, Carl Sagan, and Cold Fusion, respectively. Upon reading this tidbit of information, the real Carl Sagan fired off the following letter to *MacWEEK*:

The Power Macintosh 7100/66 was code-named Carl Sagan.

Carl's Complaint

"I have been approached many times over the past two decades by individuals and corporations seeking to use my name and/or likeness for commercial purposes. I have always declined, no matter how lucrative the offer or how important the corporation. My endorsement is not for sale. For this reason, I was profoundly distressed to see your lead front-page story 'Trio of PowerPC Macs spring toward March release date' proclaiming Apple's announcement of a new Mac bearing my name. That this was done without my authorization or knowledge is especially disturbing. Through my attorneys, I have repeatedly requested Apple to make a public clarification that I knew nothing of its intention to capitalize on my reputation in introducing this product, that I derived no benefit, financial or otherwise, from its doing so. Apple has refused. I would appreciate it if you would so apprise your readership."

Carl Sagan
Director, Laboratory for Planetary Studies
Center for Radiophysics and Space Research
Cornell University
Ithaca, NY

Sagan's letter appeared in the January 10, 1994 issue of *MacWEEK* and elicited howls of derision from the Macintosh community. Most people wondered why Sagan was complaining; he should have been honored to have a computer named after him, they felt. Besides, it was never meant to be the final product name, so lighten up.

It has been suggested that what upset Sagan the most was being grouped with two discredited scientific discoveries/hoaxes, Piltdown Man and Cold Fusion.

In deference to the noted star-gazer, Apple changed the Power Macintosh 7100/66 code name to BHA. Things were beginning to return to normal when Sagan learned that BHA supposedly stood for Butt-head Astronomer. He put pressure on Apple's lawyers, who insisted the project engineers come up with a new name. They settled on LAW, which stands for Lawyers Are Wimps. Nonetheless, in the third week of April 1994, Sagan sued Apple in U.S. District Court in Los Angeles, charging it with defamation of character. He is seeking unspecified damages, probably hoping to reap "billions and billions" of dollars.

Windows: How Sculley Betrayed the Mac

Microsoft and its boyish, multi-billionaire chairman, William Henry Gates III, are much maligned in the Macintosh community. Many Mac fanatics view Gates as the anti-Christ, stuffing inferior products down the throats of the world's computer users in an all-out effort to rule the industry and crush the Mac. Sure, Gates wants it all (he already has a darn big chunk of it), but he is absolutely not a Mac hater. In fact, he's probably the biggest fan of the Macintosh way of computing. Read on for the fascinating tale of Gates' transformation from benevolent co-conspirator to reviled competitor, and discover how Apple itself is really to blame for the success of Windows.

At Microsoft, Jeff Harbors gave the Macintosh the code name Sand, in reference to Steve Jobs' grandiose vision of Apple's Mac factory consuming raw sand at one end of the highly-automated line, turning it into silicon, and eventually churning out finished computers at the other end. Serendipitously, the code name also stood for Steve's Amazing New Device.

Steve Jobs realized that he needed the support of the third-party development community if the Mac was to be successful, so on January 22, 1982, he entered into an agreement with Gates. In return for Gates' promise to develop Mac applications, Jobs provided Microsoft with precious Mac prototypes. True to its word, Microsoft began the most extensive Mac software development effort outside of Apple, but it also turned around and began work on Windows for the IBM PC and its clones. Gates was simply hedging his bets. Although he had amassed a fortune with the command-line interface of MS-DOS, he realized that the future of the industry was in graphical user interfaces. And since Apple was writing its own Mac operating system, Gates wanted to make sure Microsoft got a piece of the action on the PC.

Courtesy of Microsoft Corp.

Bill Gates, Mac friend or foe?

245

> ## "Hey, Steve, just because you broke into Xerox's house before I did and took the TV doesn't mean I can't go in later and take the stereo."

Bill Gates, in response to Jobs complaining about how much Windows looks like the Mac

MacWEEK, March 14, 1989, p. 1

Eager to steal Jobs' thunder, Gates preannounced Windows at the Helmsley Palace Hotel in New York City on November 10, 1983, and predicted that by the end of 1984, Windows would be used on more than 90 percent of all IBM compatible computers. Just a few months later when Apple introduced the Macintosh, Gates stood proudly as a staunch supporter of the Cupertino upstarts and announced the immediate availability of MultiPlan and Microsoft BASIC. Microsoft had invested heavily in its Mac software division and was eager to reap the rewards of being first to market with many major applications that would soon follow.

> "I don't know what is going to happen to Windows, or to VisiOn, but IBM's windowing package will be the standard. We hear it is not that great, but it will be the standard."
>
> **Steve Jobs**, betting on the wrong horse
> *Personal Computing*, April 1984, p. 194

Although Gates publicly expressed high hopes for the Macintosh, privately Microsoft's Windows project steamed ahead at full speed. The difficult task of slapping a graphical user interface on top of the text-based MS-DOS was compounded by fear of being sued if the end result looked too much like the Mac. A few weeks before releasing Windows 1.01 in 1985, Microsoft was genuinely concerned that Apple was going to sue over interface similarities between Windows and the Mac, so Gates bluffed Apple CEO John Sculley with an ultimatum: call off the lawyers or Microsoft would stop development on Word and Excel for Macintosh.

"If Macintosh isn't a success, then the market is left to the PC. But we're superenthusiastic. If Apple can meet its production goals, we expect half of Microsoft's retail sales in 1984 to be Macintosh-related."

Bill Gates

Popular Science, March 1984, p. 166

This was a crucial period for Apple. The Mac was selling only 20,000 units a month, far below the initial monthly forecast of 100,000 units. Apple desperately needed the continued support of the world's largest consumer software publisher, and Gates knew it. However, Apple's top brass was convinced there was no way Microsoft would walk away from the Mac applications market which it was already dominating. They urged Sculley to stand tough, but instead, he blinked. On October 24, 1985, four days before Gates was to turn 30 years old, Sculley handed him the best birthday present ever: Apple would allow Microsoft to use some Mac technology in Windows, and in turn Microsoft would hold off shipping a Windows version of Excel for a while, giving the Mac a chance to secure a foothold in the business market.

MICROSOFT®
WINDOWS NT™

Microsoft shipped Windows on November 20, and two days later during the Fall Comdex (a huge industry trade show) in Las Vegas, Nevada, Gates and Sculley signed a confidential, three-page agreement which granted Microsoft a "non-exclusive, worldwide, royalty-free, perpetual, nontransferable license to use these derivative works in present and future software programs, and to license them to and through third parties for use in their software programs." In exchange, Apple got Microsoft's commitment to upgrade Word for Macintosh, delay Excel for Windows until October 1, 1986, plus an acknowledgment that "the visual displays in [Excel, Windows, Word, and MultiPlan] are derivative works of the visual displays generated by Apple's Lisa and Macintosh graphic user interface programs." In other words, Microsoft got Apple's crown jewels and Apple got shafted. Not since British Prime Minister Neville Chamberlain appeased Adolf Hitler with the Munich Pact of 1938 has the world seen such a fine demonstration of negotiation skills.

SEPARATED AT BIRTH?

Courtesy of The Bettmann Archive & Apple Computer, Inc.

John Sculley   Neville Chamberlain

As any computer executive will tell you, the software business is an annuities game where you sell a product once and continue to reap revenue from periodic upgrades, so an upgrade to the buggy Word was inevitable because it was in Microsoft's best interest anyway. Furthermore, Gates knew that Microsoft wouldn't be able to ship Excel for Windows before the postponement date, so the stipulation was moot. In fact, it didn't ship until October 1987. And what's the harm of acknowledging the Mac's influence on Windows in a confidential document?

"That's not what a Mac does. I want Mac on the PC, I want Mac on the PC."

Bill Gates, arguing in favor of overlapping, not tiled, windows for Microsoft Windows

Gates, p. 256

The first version of Windows didn't really catch on, but Microsoft is nothing if not persistent. Once it sets its sights on something, it keeps cranking away at it, doggedly making minor revisions and alterations. Gates loved the Mac and was slowly but surely fashioning Windows in its image. In January 1988, Microsoft released Windows 2.03, which incorporated Mac-like icons and threw aside the old tiled windows in favor of overlapping windows. The result was too close for comfort as far as Apple was concerned, and on March 17 (Saint Patrick's Day), 1988, Apple responded by filing an 11-page suit in federal court in San Jose, accusing Microsoft of infringing Apple's copyrights by producing computer programs that imitate the Lisa/Mac audiovisual works. Also named as a defendant in the suit was Hewlett-Packard, whose NewWave ran on top of Windows.

"When we were developing the Macintosh we kept in mind a famous quote of Picasso: 'Good artists copy, great artists steal.' What do I think of the suit? I personally don't understand it...Can I copyright gravity? No."

Steve Jobs, after having left Apple
Gates, p. 361

Microsoft countersued, claiming that its 1985 agreement with Apple gave it the right to use the contested features in Windows, but Apple maintained that the agreement applied to only the first version of Windows. The suit had the desired effect of instilling fear, uncertainty, and doubt in the Windows development community. As Borland's Philippe Kahn stated, it was like "waking up and finding out that your partner might have AIDS." (*Gates*, p. 361) Undeterred, Microsoft steadfastly continued updating Windows, releasing version 3.0 on May 22, 1990.

Initially, things seemed to be going in Apple's favor. Over time the court ruled that the 1985 agreement wasn't a complete defense for Microsoft, acknowledged the originality of Apple's copyrighted works, added Windows 3.0 to the complaint, and dismissed many of the counterclaims. But on August 14, 1991, the tide turned when the court reconsidered the originality of Apple's audiovisual display. On April 14, 1992, the court substantially narrowed the scope of the issues when it held that most of the Windows and NewWave interface elements were either covered by the 1985 license or could not be protected under copyright law. Finally the whole enchilada was decided in Microsoft's favor on August 24, 1993 when the court dismissed Apple's action.

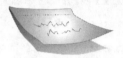

Ironically, after Apple successfully sued Franklin Computer Corporation in 1983 for copying its read-only memory code in order to sell Apple II clones, Gates himself lauded the outcome in an opinion piece for *The New York Times* business section: "Imagine the disincentive to software development if after months of work another company could come along and copy your work and market it under its own name... Without legal restraints on such copying, companies like Apple could not afford to advance the state of the art."

The ruling was a mere technicality at that point because a much-improved Windows 3.1 had by then come to dominate the personal computer marketplace, with Apple's Mac share hovering around 15 percent. To this day the full damage of the 1985 agreement remains difficult to assess. Had Apple held its ground, Microsoft may not have grown as powerful as it has. Now, almost ten years after Sculley caved in to Gates' demands, Apple has announced its intention to port the Mac operating system to Intel-based platforms where it will have to compete head-to-head with Microsoft's Windows 4.0 (code-named Chicago) which promises to be much more Mac-like than ever. Keep your eyes open, this promises to be an interesting fight.

252

Windows Timeline

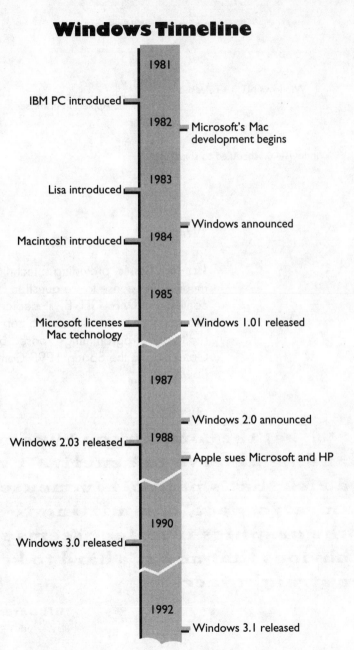

	1981
IBM PC introduced	
	1982 — Microsoft's Mac development begins
Lisa introduced	**1983**
	— Windows announced
Macintosh introduced	**1984**
	1985
Microsoft licenses Mac technology	— Windows 1.01 released
	1987
	— Windows 2.0 announced
Windows 2.03 released	**1988**
	— Apple sues Microsoft and HP
	1990
Windows 3.0 released	
	1992
	— Windows 3.1 released

Windows Timeline

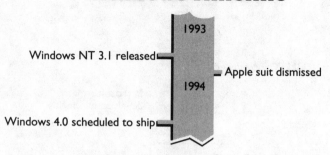

Windows NT 3.1 released — 1993

— Apple suit dismissed

1994

Windows 4.0 scheduled to ship —

"Windows."

Jean-Louis Gassée, providing a technically incorrect response to the question "What contest, held via USENET, is dedicated to examples of weird, obscure, bizarre, and really bad programming?" posed by Bill Gates during the Spring 1993 Computer Bowl

"We bet the company on Windows and we deserve to benefit. It was a risk that's paid off immensely. In retrospect, committing to the graphics interface seems so obvious that now it's hard to keep a straight face.

Bill Gates

Playboy, July 1994, p. 62

254

Jobs after Apple: NeXT to NoTHING

After being stripped of all operational responsibilities on May 31, 1985, Jobs had little to do at Apple, so he began canvassing the country's colleges asking them to describe their ideal university computer. In early September, Jobs had lunch with Paul Berg, Nobel laureate and Stanford University biochemist. When Berg complained of the difficulty of performing "wet lab" research on gene splicing, Jobs suggested simulating the experiments on a computer. Berg was supposedly so enthusiastic about the idea that Jobs realized he was on to something big. Within weeks Jobs decided to found a start-up with five other Apple employees: Susan Barnes (senior controller for U.S. sales and marketing), George Crow (engineering manager), Dan'l Lewin (higher education marketing manager), Rich Page (Apple Fellow), and Bud Tribble (manager of software engineering).

"I feel like somebody just punched me in the stomach and knocked all my wind out. I'm only 30 years old and I want to have a chance to continue creating things."

Steve Jobs, on being stripped of an operating role at Apple
Playboy, September 1987, p. 53

255

> **"Our minds are sort of like electro-chemical computers. Your thoughts construct patterns like scaffolding in your mind. You are really etching chemical patterns. In most cases, people get stuck in those patterns, just like grooves in a record, and they never get out of them. It's a rare person who etches grooves that are other than a specific way of looking at things, a specific way of questioning things. It's rare that you see an artist in his 30s or 40s able to really contribute something amazing."**
>
> **Steve Jobs**
>
> *Playboy*, February 1985, p. 58

When Jobs announced his plans to Apple's board of directors, it initially expressed an interest in investing in the new venture, Next Inc. (later changed to NeXT Computer, Inc.), but the board went ballistic when Jobs revealed the names of the five employees who would be joining him. Jobs resigned as Apple chairman, and Apple sued him for dereliction of duties. Apple eventually dropped the suit in January 1986 when Jobs agreed to a six-month moratorium on hiring Apple employees. Curiously, Apple insisted on a non-compete clause that required any computers created by Jobs' new company to be more powerful than any of Apple's offerings.

How to Blow $817 Million

At the time he left Apple, Jobs owned roughly 6.5 million shares of stock, or about 11.3 percent of the company. Over the course of the year, Jobs began liquidating his massive holdings at what would prove to be fire sale prices. According to Securities and Exchange Commission records, Jobs dumped 4.028 million shares in 1985 for $70.5 million. By February 1986, Jobs claimed to have sold all but one share so that he would still receive Apple's annual reports. Assuming this is true and that he managed to sell at the highest price realized by February, the most he could have grossed was $135 million. As it turns out, Jobs couldn't have picked a worse time to sell his Apple stock.

To be sure, Jobs needed some seed money for his new start-up company, but he could have made do with the proceeds from selling just a fraction of his Apple position (his initial investment in NeXT was just $7 million). And his assertion that he was selling because he had lost faith in Apple's executives is certainly a valid reason. But, boy, did he suffer from poor timing! Had he held on until the 2-for-1 split in April 1987, he would have been sitting on 13 million shares, worth $776 million when the stock peaked that October, or $952 million when the stock reached its all-time high in April 1991. Not counting dividends, Jobs left over $817 million on the table when he cashed out of Apple. Man, that's gotta hurt!

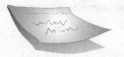

For the first four months of its life, NeXT operated out of Jobs' Woodside mansion at 460 Mountain Home Road (the iron-gated entrance is actually on Robles Drive). The first formal offices were in the Stanford University Industrial Park in Palo Alto, not far from Xerox PARC. The company eventually moved to an office complex in Redwood City, where it is located today.

Even though he was successful in recruiting top talent, Jobs was way off base when he originally predicted that NeXT would produce a machine by the spring of 1987. As it turned out, it wasn't until October 12, 1988 that Jobs unveiled the NeXT Computer to the anxious crowd of 4,500 assembled at Louise M. Davies Symphony Hall in San Francisco. Even that was premature because the final version of the NEXTSTEP operating system (originally called NeXTstep) didn't ship until September 18, 1989. Still, Jobs didn't see the NeXT Computer as late, but rather, "five years ahead of its time."

©NeXT Computer, Inc.

The NeXT Computer got glowing reviews upon introduction.

258

> "Develop for it? I'll piss on it."
>
> **Bill Gates**, Microsoft chairman, in response to *InfoWorld's* Peggy Watt asking if Microsoft would develop applications for the NeXT Computer
>
> *Accidental Empires*, p. 311

The specifications certainly were impressive: 25-megahertz (MHz) Motorola 68030 processor, 8 megabytes (MB) of main memory expandable to 16 MB, 250-MB Canon optical disc drive, Motorola 6882 math coprocessor, and Motorola 56001 digital signal processor to drive real-time sound, array processing, modem, fax, and encryption functions. All this was housed in a cube 12 inches on each side, with a 17-inch Sony monochrome monitor, keyboard, and mouse. The NeXT Computer ran a Unix 4.3-based Mach operating system and featured a powerful object-oriented development environment. Also included on disc was the complete works of Shakespeare, a dictionary, thesaurus, book of quotations, documentation, WriteNow, Mathematica, a relational database server, an artificial intelligence language, a C compiler, personal information manager, and graphical electronic mail with integrated voice capabilities.

NeXT announced that it would sell the entire package direct to colleges and universities, which would in turn resell them to students and faculty for $6,500. (At the time, Apple's top-of-the-line computer was the Mac IIx, with a 16-MHz 68030 and a suggested retail price of $7,769 for a stripped-down model.)

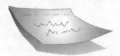

When describing the NeXT Computer, the press never failed to make a big deal about the unique black matte finish of the 12-inch cube, calling it a bold new look. Actually, Jobs had his hand in designing another black computer years ago. In the summer of 1981, Apple produced a special version of the Apple II for the audio-visual equipment manufacturer, Bell & Howell. It was distinguished from the standard Apple II by extra audio and video connectors on the back panel and its all-black plastic housing. Also interesting to note is that the same industrial design firm—Hartmut Esslinger's frogdesign—responsible for the big, black NeXT Computer was also responsible for the sleek "Snow White" Apple IIc introduced in 1984.

Like the Macintosh before it, the NeXT Computer took longer than expected to develop, was more expensive than originally hoped for, used a non-standard disk drive, and did not have a color display. Nonetheless, the initial press reaction was enormously favorable. Stewart Alsop, editor of *P.C. Letter*, predicted that NeXT would sell 25,000 machines in 18 months. Michael Murphy, editor of *California Technology Stock Letter*, went one better in predicting that NeXT would sell 50,000 machines in two years. And Louise Kohl, executive editor at *MacUser*, predicted "This machine will replace sex."

When all the hoopla of the introduction faded, it became apparent that higher education just didn't see things the

same way as the fawning press. The NeXT Computer didn't deliver what the educators had asked for. It was too expensive to be a personal computer, and too underpowered to be a workstation, leading NeXT's marketing staff to invent the term "personal workstation" so that it could claim to be a leader in a market segment that heretofore didn't exist.

The Best Logo Money Can Buy

Nobody has ever accused Steve Jobs of frugality. When it came to choosing a logo for his new company, Jobs spared no expense. He met with four noted designers, but none was deemed worthy. Ultimately, Jobs decided he wanted 71-year-old, Yale professor Paul Rand to design the NeXT logo. Rand, widely considered the grand master of American graphics arts, had previously designed logos for such business institutions as United Parcel Service, Westinghouse, ABC television, and IBM. In fact, it was Rand who, in the 1960s, convinced International Business Machines to drop its full name and use only initials. Rand continued to consult for IBM, so initially he declined to work on a logo for Jobs, citing a conflict of interest. Amazingly enough, Jobs convinced IBM vice chairman Paul Rizzo to release Rand of his obligation.

SEPARATED AT BIRTH?

©NeXT Computer, Inc.

Perhaps Rand had heard about how mercurial Jobs could be, because before accepting the commission, he insisted on being paid $100,000 in advance to create only one design, and he would be under no obligation to revise his work if it failed to please Jobs. Jobs accepted the terms and in June 1986, Rand produced a logo reminiscent of a child's wooden block tilted at a precise 28° angle, bearing the letters of the company, each in a different color, perhaps inspired by artist Robert Indiana's Love painting that was popularized by an 8¢ postage stamp released on January 26, 1973. The bizarre capitalization of the company's name was Rand's idea, who explained that the lower-case e would stand out and could represent "education, excellence, expertise, exceptional, excitement, e=mc²."

As soon as it became apparent that NeXT wasn't going to be successful selling only to higher education, it struck a deal with Businessland, giving the nation's largest computer retailer the rights to sell 100,000 machines in three years. At the March 1989 announcement, Businessland's chairman, president, and CEO David Norman boldly predicted that "NeXT revenues will be as much over the next twelve months as Compaq was over the last twelve months. Compaq business was about $150 million."

Considering that Businessland would sell the computer for $9,995, with absolutely no discounting, Norman's boast worked out to roughly 10,000 machines, plus peripherals, in the coming year. While that may not seem like an unrealistic goal, consider that toward the end of 1988, NeXT was selling a pathetic 400 machines a month at the educator's price of $6,500. Oblivious to the clear signals the marketplace was sending, NeXT's head of manufacturing was ramping up the factory to produce 120,000 computers annually.

The NeXTstation addressed many of the faults of its predecessor

Humbled by the underwhelming response to the NeXT
Computer, Jobs and company set about addressing some
of the major complaints about its speed, price, lack of
color, hard drives, and floppies. On September 18, 1990,
NeXT introduced a series of new workstations based on
the brand-new, 25-MHz Motorola 68040 processor. The
$4,995 NeXTstation, or "slab," was shaped like a pizza
box containing a 2.88-MB, 3.5-inch floppy disk drive, a
105-MB hard disk, 8 MB of memory expandable to 32
MB, and a monochrome monitor.

The $7,995 NeXTstation Color came with a 16-inch
MegaPixel Trinitron monitor capable of displaying 4,096
colors, sound box, and memory expandable from 12 MB
to 32 MB. The $7,995 NeXTcube, housed in a case similar
to the original NeXT Computer, came standard with the
same display, memory, and disk configuration as the
NeXTstation, but since it was designed to be a network
server, it offered more expansion possibilities in those
areas. For an additional $3,995, users could add the 32-bit

NeXTdimension video board giving the NeXTcube 16.7 million colors in Display PostScript. (By way of comparison, the best Apple had to offer at the time was the $8,969 Mac IIfx with a 40-MHz 68030.)

Five Founders Flee

Person	Position at NeXT	Departure	Destination
Susan Barnes	CFO	04/91	Richard Blum & Associates
George Crow	VP of analog engineering	04/93	na
Dan'l Lewin	VP of marketing	02/90	Kaleida Labs
Rich Page	VP of hardware	01/93	start-up
Bud Tribble	VP of software	06/92	Sun Microsystems

To outward appearances, NeXT was on a roll, but looks were deceiving. The '040-based machines didn't ship for months after their introduction due to a shortage of the new processors from Motorola. Furthermore, the NeXTdimension's compression chip was abandoned by its third-party developer, leaving an empty socket on the board and a bad taste in the mouths of true believers who had spent almost $12,000 for the high-end color system. In April 1991, another founder, Susan Barnes, called it quits. Then on May 14, NeXT was forced to terminate its March 1989 sales agreement with Businessland because the retailer closed its outlets. To make matters worse, the firm's highly-respected outside investor, H. Ross Perot, resigned from the board of directors in June, complaining "I shouldn't have let you guys have all that money. Biggest mistake I made."

At the first NeXTWORLD Expo held in San Francisco on January 22, 1992, Jobs announced cheaper, faster, "Turbo"

versions of the NeXTstation, NeXTstation Color, and NeXTcube, all built around the 33-MHz Motorola 68040 processor. More significantly, he announced NEXTSTEP 3.0 and NEXTSTEP 486, a $995 version that would run on Intel 80486 processors simultaneously with Unix, MS-DOS, and Windows. NEXTSTEP 3.0 was to ship in the second quarter of 1992, but didn't make it out the door until late September. NEXTSTEP 486 was originally promised for September, but didn't ship until May 1993. By then the name had changed to NEXTSTEP For Intel Processors since it could run on both 486 and Pentium machines.

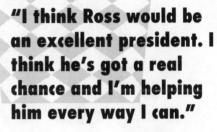

"I think Ross would be an excellent president. I think he's got a real chance and I'm helping him every way I can."

Steve Jobs

NeXTWORLD, Fall 1992, p. 33

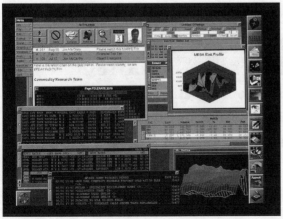

©NeXT Computer, Inc.

NeXT is pinning its hopes on the NEXTSTEP object-oriented operating system for Intel-based computers.

> "Medicine will cure death and government will repeal taxes before Steve will fail. You can quote me."
>
> **Guy Kawasaki**, former Apple evangelist, explaining why NeXT will eclipse Sun Microsystems as the dominant workstation manufacturer
>
> *NeXTWORLD*, Fall 1991, p. 80

Realizing he could never recreate the magic necessary to make Silicon Valley's next Apple Computer, Jobs decided to shoot for becoming the next Microsoft. On February 10, 1993—"Black Tuesday"—NeXT laid off 280 of its 530 employees and announced it would sell the hardware side of its business to Canon so that it could focus on selling NEXTSTEP as the premier object-oriented operating system for Intel-based computers.

"Without Jobs, Apple is just another Silicon Valley company, and without Apple, Jobs is just another Silicon Valley millionaire."

Nick Arnett, high-tech journalist

Accidental Millionaire, p. 218

NeXT Timeline

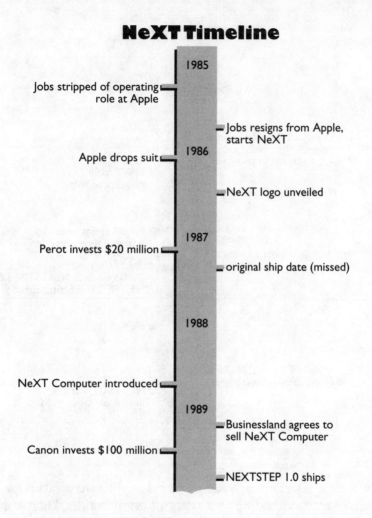

1985

Jobs stripped of operating role at Apple

Jobs resigns from Apple, starts NeXT

1986

Apple drops suit

NeXT logo unveiled

1987

Perot invests $20 million

original ship date (missed)

1988

NeXT Computer introduced

1989

Businessland agrees to sell NeXT Computer

Canon invests $100 million

NEXTSTEP 1.0 ships

NeXT Timeline

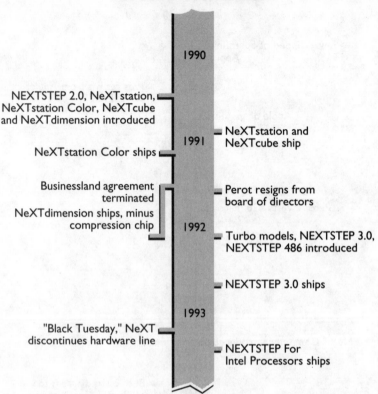

1990

NEXTSTEP 2.0, NeXTstation, NeXTstation Color, NeXTcube and NeXTdimension introduced

1991 — NeXTstation and NeXTcube ship

NeXTstation Color ships

Businessland agreement terminated

— Perot resigns from board of directors

NeXTdimension ships, minus compression chip

1992 — Turbo models, NEXTSTEP 3.0, NEXTSTEP 486 introduced

— NEXTSTEP 3.0 ships

1993

"Black Tuesday," NeXT discontinues hardware line

— NEXTSTEP For Intel Processors ships

While NEXTSTEP is widely considered to be a fabulous product, the market is not without competition. Microsoft's own object-oriented version of Windows NT (code-named Cairo) is scheduled for release in 1994, and both IBM and Apple have high hopes for Pink, the operating system under development at their joint venture, Taligent. Although his hardware failures have tarnished his image

268

as Silicon Valley's golden boy, few people are willing to write off Jobs altogether, and many secretly wish he can pull off another miracle to match the Mac. Keep your fingers crossed.

It took Apple only 73 days to sell 50,000 Macintosh computers. It took Jobs five years to sell as many NeXT computers.

"You can have a good product with a lot of good philosophical thinking behind it—a lot of pureness—and still not sell. You gotta have some luck, too. The NeXT is a good machine that just didn't have the luck to make it successful."

Steve Wozniak

"There are a lot of people who do one incredible thing and then we never hear from them again. J. D. Salinger wrote *Catcher in the Rye*, but what else has he done?"

Deborah Coleman, former controller of the Mac division, explaining Jobs' NeXT failure
Forbes, April 29, 1991

269

The Money Trail

NeXT began life in 1985 with a $7 million stake from Jobs, but was operating at a ferocious burn rate that would leave it penniless by the end of 1986. Rather than dig into his own pockets again, Jobs distributed a prospectus throughout the venture capital community that he had spurned when NeXT was founded. Now Jobs was only too willing to accept their investments. He sought $3 million for a 10 percent stake in NeXT, giving the productless, revenueless NeXT a ludicrous $30 million valuation. Not surprisingly, there were no takers.

As luck would have it, H. Ross Perot was watching television one night in November 1986 when he came across John Nathan's "The Entrepreneurs," a documentary in which NeXT was featured. Perot was so fascinated by the young start-up that he called Jobs the following day and casually remarked "If you ever need an investor, call me." (*Life*, February 1988, p. 70) Not wanting to appear anxious, Jobs waited a week before inviting Perot to come take a look at his firm and meet its employees. Instead of focusing on the hard-and-fast numbers which would never stand up to due diligence, Jobs insisted Perot consider the intangibles. The approached appealed to Perot, who essentially opened his checkbook and asked Jobs how much he wanted.

Apparently Jobs was running a very special sale that day reserved just for diminutive billionaire Texans. Jobs demanded $20 million for 16 percent of NeXT, giving the firm an unbelievable valuation of $125 million. In February 1987, Perot accepted without blinking and became the company's largest investor and a board member. "Do the math," said one venture capitalist, "and you have to assume that Perot is investing more out of emotion than prudence." Perot justified the

price by responding, "I'm investing in quality." (*Newsweek*, February 9, 1987, p. 48)

Perot got a bargain compared to Canon. In June 1989, the Japanese conglomerate paid $100 million for a 16.67 percent share of NeXT, giving the company an implicit value of $600 million. By the time NeXT dropped its hardware in February 1993, Perot had trimmed his stake to 11 percent, leaving Canon with its 16.67 percent and Jobs as the majority share-holder with 46 percent of outstanding shares.

"He told me that we're going to hit one out of the ball park."

Steve Jobs, after future presidential wanna-be H. Ross Perot invested in NeXT
Accidental Millionaire, p. 214

Macintosh Insiders: Where Are They Now?

If you've ever cracked open the case of an early Macintosh, you may have noticed a bunch of signatures in raised plastic on the inside back panel. Steve Jobs felt that the Macintosh was a piece of art, and since real artists sign their masterpieces, he and the other employees of the Macintosh division in 1982 affixed their signatures to a large sheet of paper. When everyone had signed, a film negative was made from the paper, and the signatures were chemically etched into the core of the tooling for the inside of the original Macintosh.

 Apple continued using the same case mold until it finally wore out sometime during the production of the Mac SE, at which time a signature-free mold was substituted.

Here's a brief look at the people who created the Mac and an update on what they were doing "now," defined as January 24, 1994, the tenth anniversary of the Mac's introduction (Silicon Valley is infamous for its burn'n' turn approach to human resources, so don't be surprised if people are no longer at the companies listed).

Mac fanatics will no doubt notice the absence of some prestigious members of the Mac division, such as Steve

Capps and Susan Kare. They weren't left out on purpose. It's just that they weren't on the team when the signatures were collected in early 1982, a time when Steve Jobs felt that shipping was imminent. Of course, it was almost two years too soon, but almost everything about the Mac was ahead of its time.

Please note that some signatures were added (such as Steve Balog) over time and others were dropped (ostensibly to accommodate changes in the case design for the Mac SE). The signatures shown here are as they appear on the original master.

Peggy Alexio

Then: Area associate

Now: Whereabouts unknown

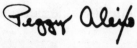

Collette Askeland

Then: Designed the printed circuit board for the main logic board

Now: Managing the computer-aided-design support staff at Apple

Bill Atkinson

Then: Wrote QuickDraw and MacPaint

Now: Left Apple in 1990; chief technologist at General Magic

Robert L. Belleville

Then: Engineering manager

Now: Left Apple in 1986; corporate R&D department of Silicon Graphics

Mike Boich

Then: Software evangelist

Now: Left Apple in 1985; chairman of Radius

Bill Bull

Then: Worked on the "no-fan solution" decreed by Jobs, plus the cables, keyboard, and mouse

Now: Manager of product design for Apple Business Systems

Matt Carter

Then: In charge of the Macintosh factory

Now: Left Apple in 1983; starting a new company

Berry Cash

Then: Marketing and sales consultant

Now: Left project in 1983; venture capitalist in Texas

Debi Coleman

Debi Coleman
Then: Controller of the Macintosh division
Now: Left Apple in 1992; VP of materials operations
at Tektronix

George Crow

George Crow
Then: Designed the analog board, video, and power
supply
Now: Left Apple in 1985; director of central
engineering at SuperMac

Donn Denman

Donn Denman
Then: Wrote Alarm Clock and NotePad desk
accessories and MacBASIC
Now: Apple Solution Tools Group programmer
(AppleScript)

Christopher Espinosa

Then: Supervised the writing of the manuals and technical documentation

Now: Works at Apple on the Apple-IBM relationship and runs the project offices for Taligent and Kaleida

Bill Fernandez

Then: Engineering jack-of-all-trades
Now: Left Apple in 1993; consulting

Martin P. Haeberli

Then: Worked on the Memory Manager and co-authored MacTerminal

Now: Manager of Technology Assessment for Apple's higher education business unit

Andy Hertzfeld

Andy Hertzfeld

Then: Software wizard; wrote most of the Macintosh Toolbox

Now: Left Apple in 1985; VP and programmer at General Magic

Joanna Karin Hoffman

Joanna K. Hoffman

Then: Wrote the first marketing plan for the division

Now: Left Apple in 1985; VP of marketing at General Magic

Rod Holt

Rod Holt

Then: Worked on the power supply

Now: Left Apple in 1987; retired and sailing boats

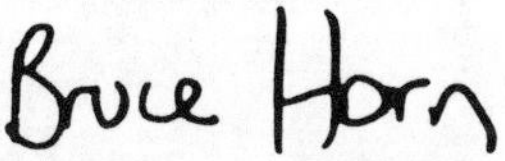

Bruce Horn

Bruce Horn

Then: Designed the Finder and completed it with Steve Capps

Now: Left Apple in 1984; finished doctorate in computer science at Carnegie Mellon University

Hap Horn

Harrison S. Horn

Then: Linear circuit designer

Now: Left Apple in 1983; retired, living in Los Altos

Brian R. Howard

Brian R. Howard

Then: Ensured that the digital designs would work and be manufacturable

Now: Engineer in the portable computing division of Apple

Steven Jobs

Then: General manager of the division

Now: Left Apple in 1985; CEO of NeXT Computer, Inc.

Larry Kenyon

Then: Worked on the file system, drivers, and boot code

Now: Programmer in the Newton group at Apple

Patti King

Then: Managed the engineering department's software library

Now: Left Apple in 1985; full-time mom, married to Larry Kenyon

Daniel Kottke

Daniel Kottke

Then: Built prototypes and troubleshot board-level problems

Now: Left Apple in 1985; father's rights activist and head of Pollstar, a hardware start-up

Angeline Lo

Then: Programmer

Now: Left Apple in 1982; whereabouts unknown

Ivan Mach

Then: Optimized main logic and power sweep boards for factory automation

Now: Left Apple in 1984; director of manufacturing for WiSE, a wireless start-up

Jerrold C. Manock

Jerrold C. Manock

Then: Managed the industrial design engineers

Now: Left Apple in 1985; running an industrial design company in Vermont

M.E. McCammon

Mary Ellen McCammon

Then: Area associate for the marketing people

Now: Left Apple in 1986; completing a master's degree in psychology

Vicki Milledge

Vicki Milledge

Then: Human resources

Now: Left Apple in 1988; whereabouts unknown

Michael R. Murray

Then: Director of marketing

Now: Left Apple in 1985; VP of human resources and administration at Microsoft

Ronald H. Nicholson Jr.

Then: Digital hardware engineer

Now: Left Apple in 1983; engineer at Rich Page's Sierra Research & Technology

Terry A. Oyama

Then: Worked on the product design of housing

Now: Left Apple in 1985; industrial design manager at Radius

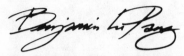

Benjamin Pang

Then: Worked on the industrial design of Macintosh
Now: Industrial designer at Apple

Jef Raskin

Then: Father of the original Macintosh project in 1979
Now: Left Apple in 1982; human interface design consultant and writer

Ed Riddle

Then: Worked on the design of the keyboard
Now: Left Apple in 1981; writer in the areas of technical, marketing, and spiritual issues

Brian Robertson

Then: Managed purchasing and supplier sourcing

Now: Director of Macintosh product operations at Apple

David H. Roots

Then: Worked on the product design of keyboard, external disk drive

Now: Left Apple in 1989; senior product designer at Radius

Patricia Sharp

Then: Steve Jobs' administrative assistant

Now: In charge of staffing and development functions at Apple

Burrell Carver Smith

Then: Designed the digital board, and was the division's hardware wizard

Now: Left Apple in 1985; doing research in Palo Alto

Bryan Stearns

Then: Worked on the user interface for MacBASIC

Now: Developing Apple's Newton programming tools

Lynn Takahashi

Then: Steve Jobs' area associate

Now: Left Apple in 1985; manager of marketing programs at General Magic

Guy L. Tribble III

Then: Manager of software engineering

Now: Left Apple in 1985; VP at SunSoft, the software subsidiary of Sun Microsystems

Randy Wigginton

Then: Wrote MacWrite on contract

Now: Left Apple in 1981; software engineer at Eo Inc., a Santa Clara computer firm

Linda Wilkin

Then: Managed engineering documentation

Now: Left Apple in 1986; operations manager at Clarify, a San Jose software company

Steve Wozniak

Then: A few weeks after joining the Mac team, Steve crashed his plane and had to drop out. Nonetheless, he was such an inspiration to Burrell Smith and Andy Hertzfeld that they insisted he sign the case despite the fact that Woz admits "I wasn't a critical part of the team."

Now: Teaching fifth graders how to use computers at UNUSON in Los Gatos

Pamela G. Wyman

Then: User manual designer/production editor

Now: Left Apple in 1985; end-user assistance and training designer for Windows at Microsoft

Laszlo Zsidek

Then: Tooling and manufacturing engineer

Now: Works in the portable computing division of Apple

Thanks to Guy Kawasaki for the initial research upon which this piece is based.

Alternative Apples

Apple is pretty laid back when it comes to corporate formalities such as business titles. To be sure, the company's personnel department keeps track of positions using normal titles, but employees are given a lot of latitude in deciding how they present themselves to the outside world. Here's just a sampling of some funky titles on actual Apple business cards I've accumulated over the years:

Allen J. Baum: Chief Wirehead

Mike Boich: Software Evangelist

Frank Casanova II: Lord of High End Mac

Donn Denman: Crank Inventor

Steve Goldberg: 7.0 Guy

Martin Haeberli: Hardware Wizard of Macintosh

Andy Hertsfeld: Software Artist, Macintosh Software Wizard

Don Louv: Wild Newt Tamer

John Sculley: Chief Listener

Burrell Smith: Hardware Wizard

Bibliography

Butcher, Lee. *Accidental Millionaire: The Rise and Fall of Steve Jobs at Apple Computer.* New York, NY: Paragon House Publishers, 1988.

Cohen, Scott. *Zap!: The Rise and Fall of Atari.* New York, NY: Osborne/McGraw-Hill Book Co., 1984.

Cringely, Robert X. *Accidental Empires: How the Boys of Silicon Valley Make Their Millions, Battle Foreign Competition, and Still Can't Get a Date.* Reading, MA: Addison-Wesley Publishing Co., 1992.

Freiberger, Paul and Michael Swaine. *Fire in the Valley.* New York, NY: Obsborne/McGraw-Hill, 1984.

Gassée, Jean-Louie. *The Third Apple: Personal Computers & the Cultural Revolution.* Orlando, FL: Harcourt Brace Jovanovich, Publishers, 1985.

Goldberg, Adele. *A History of Personal Workstations.* New York, NY: ACM Press, 1988.

Kawasaki, Guy. *The Macintosh Way: The Art of Guerrilla Management.* New York: HarperPerennial, 1990.

Kawasaki, Guy. *Selling the Dream: How to Promote Your Product, Company, or Ideas—and Make a Difference—Using Everyday Evangelism.* New York, NY: HarperCollins Publishers, 1991.

Kounalakis, Markos and Doug Menuez. *Defying Gravity: The Making of Newton*. Hillsboro, OR: Beyond Words Publishing, Inc., 1993.

LeVitus, Bob and Michael Fraase. *Guide to the Macintosh Underground: Mac Culture from the Inside*. Indianapolis, IN: Hayden Books, 1993.

Levy, Steven. *Insanely Great: The Life and Times of Macintosh, The Computer That Changed Everything*. New York, NY: Penguin Books USA Inc., 1994.

Malone, Michael S. *The Big Score*. Garden City, NY: Doubleday & Co., Inc., 1985.

Manes, Stephen and Paul Andrews. *Gates: How Microsoft's Mogul Reinvented an Industry—And Made Himself the Richest Man in America*. New York, NY: Doubleday, 1993.

Moritz, Michael. *The Little Kingdom: The Private Story of Apple Computer*. New York, NY: William Morrow and Company, Inc., 1984.

Price, Rob. *So Far: The First Ten Years of a Vision*. Cupertino, CA: Apple Computer, Inc., 1987.

Rose, Frank. *West of Eden: The End of Innocence at Apple Computer*. New York, NY: Viking Penguin Inc., 1989.

Sculley, John C. and John A. Byrne. *Odyssey: Pepsi to Apple...A journey of adventure, ideas and the future*. New York, NY: Harper & Row, Publishers, 1987.

Stross, Randall E. *Steve Jobs & the NeXT Big Thing*. New York, NY: Atheneum Macmillan Publishing Co., 1993.

Wallace, James and Jim Erickson. *Hard Drive: Bill Gates and the Making of the Microsoft Empire*. TK: John Wiley & Sons, Inc., 1992.

Young, Jeffrey S. *Steve Jobs: The Journey Is the Reward*. Glenview, IL: Scott, Foresman and Company, 1988.

Index

Note to the Reader: **Boldfaced** numbers indicate the principal discussion of a topic or the definition of a term. *Italic* numbers indicate illustrations.

Numbers

4th Dimension software, 189
1984 commercial, 109, **114–126**. *See also*
    Lemmings commercial
  airing of, 120–123
  Big Brother's speech, 125–126, *125*
  Jobs and, 114, 116, 117–118,
    120,123
  and Macintosh price, 109
  origin of, 114–115
  Ridley Scott and, 117, 125
  Sculley and, 116, 117–119, 122
  storyboard, 115–116, *115*, *116*
  Wozniak and, 120
6502 microprocessor, 15
6809E microprocessor, 93, 96
68000 microprocessor, 93, 96–97, 105

A

Abacus Concepts, 188
ACI (Analyses Conseils Informations), 189
ACIUS, 189
addresses, author's, 237
Adobe Systems, 189
Advanced Gravis, 190
advertising. *See also 1984* commercial
  Lemmings commercial, **146–150**,
    147, *148*
  in *Newsweek*, 124
After Dark software, 183
agreements. *See* license agreements
Aldus Corporation, 190–191
Alexio, Peggy, 273
Alley, Lynn and Steve, 197
Alsop, Stewart, 260
Alto computer, 60–65, *61*

Altsys Corporation, 191–192
Ambrosia Software, 192
American Express card, Bill Gates', 142–144
Analyses Conseils Informations (ACI), 189
Annie code name, 84, 86
"Any" key, 179
Apple Computer
  Apple 32 SuperMicro division, 75
  versus Apple Corps, 238–239
  becomes Fortune 500 company, 46
  corporate titles, **289**
  creation of logo, 8–9
  develop magazine, 216, 224, 226
  founding of, **1–7**, *1*, 37–38, 83
  growth of, **46**
  IBM alliance, **56–58**, *57*
  and IBM PC, **47–54**
  initial public offering (IPO), 37–38, 41,
    42, 93
  and Microsoft Corporation, 56, 57
  origin of name, **193**, 238
  stock options, **37–43**
  stock price history, **45**
  stock symbols, 44
Apple Corps, 238–239
Apple I computer
  Atari and, 12–13
  Hewlett-Packard and, 11
  price of, 155
  production of first order, 3–6, *5*, 37
Apple II computer
  and *1984* commercial, 114–115
  versus Apple III, 29
  BASIC and, 20–21
  for Bell & Howell, 260
  creation of, **14–15**
  Franklin Computer Corporation
    lawsuit, 252
  Jobs and, 14–15, 260

limitations of, 87
trademark dispute, 239
VisiCalc and, 18, 47
Apple III computer, **28–34**, *28*
Apple III Plus computer, **35–36**
Apple University Consortium, Wheels for
the Mind promotion, 94, *94*
AppleFax modem Easter eggs, 227–228
ApplePrices, 136
Applesoft BASIC, 19–20
Arnett, Nick, 266
articles. *See* magazine articles
Ashton-Tate Corporation, 189
Askeland, Collette, 273
Atari Corporation
and Apple I computer, 12–13
Breakout video game, 22–24
Atkinson, Bill
and Lisa computer, 62–63, 66, 68
and Macintosh project, 91–92, 97, 106,
106
profile, 274
and Venice font, 224

Big Idea Group (BIG), 240–241
Big Mac project, 164
Blackbird code name, 137
Blue Meanies, 234, 236
Boich, Mike, 107, 206, 274, 289
bomb icon, 184
Brainerd, Paul, 190–191
Breakout video game, 22–24
Bricklin, Daniel, 16–19, *17*
Bringhurst, Gary and Ken, 211–212
Broderbund Software, Inc., 194–195
Brown, Don, 195
Bull, Bill, 275
Bull, Vic, 214
Bunnell, David, 133
Burke, Mary, 223
Bushnell, Nolan K., 6, 22, 23
business card titles, **289**
Businessland Corporation, 262, 264
Butt-head Astronomer (BHA) code
name, 243
Byte magazine, 127–128
Byte Shop, 3–5, *3*

B

Balloon Help menu Easter eggs, 228
Balog, Steve, 273
Barnes, Susan, 164, 255, 264
BASIC, **19–21**, 246. *See also* MacBASIC
Apple II and, 20–21
Applesoft BASIC, 19–20
MacBASIC, **19–21**
Microsoft BASIC, 19–21, 246
Baudin, Jeff, 203
Baudville Corporation, 194
Baum, Allen J., 289
Belleville, Robert L., 66, 274
de Berardinis, Olivia, 232
Berg, Paul, 255
BHA (Butt-head Astronomer) code
name, 243
Bicycle code name, 94
Biedny, David, 206
Big Brother. See *1984* commercial

C

Cache Switch control panel Easter eggs, 228
caffeine, **185–187**
Cairo code name, 268
Calculedger software, 16–18
California Technology Stock Letter, 260
Campbell, Bill, 119–120
Canon Corporation
Cat word processor, 112–113, *112*
and NeXT computer, 266, 271
Canter, Marc, 202
Capps, Steve, 66, 97, 106, 272–273
Caps Lock file icon Easter eggs, 228
Carl Sagan code name, 241–243
Carlston, Don, Doug, and Gary, 194–195
Carter, Gene, 46
Carter, Matt, 206, 275
Casado, John, 83
Casanova, Frank, II, 289
Caserta, Peter, 169, 170–171

Cash, Berry, 275
Cat word processor, 112–113, *112*
CD-ROMs, 184
CE Software, 195
Chiat, Jay, 119, 149
Chiat/Day advertising agency
 and *1984* commercial, **114–119**,
  121, 123
 and *Lemmings* commercial, **146–150**,
  147, *148*
Chicago code name, 252
chips. See microprocessors
Clarus, 223–224. *See also* dogcow icon
closing windows, 179
Clow, Lee, 115, 122
code names, **25–27**. *See also* names
 Annie, 84, 86
 BHA (Butt-head Astronomer), 243
 Bicycle, 94
 Blackbird, 137
 Cairo, 268
 Carl Sagan, 241–243
 Chicago, 252
 Clarus, 223–224
 Cold Fusion, 241, 243
 Derringer, 228
 Lawyers Are Wimps (LAW), 243
 Lisa, 25, **79–80**
 Midas, 137
 Pepsi, 80
 Piltdown Man (PDM), 241, 243
 Pink, 56–58, 268
 for PowerBook, 228
 for projects, **25–27**
 Sand, 244
 Sara, 28
 Silver Surfer, 189
 Spruce Goose, 137
 TIM, 228
 Twiggy, 72
coffee, caffeine in, 187
Cold Fusion code name, 241, 243
Coleman, Deborah, 269, 276
Color control panel Easter eggs, 229
commercials. See also *1984* commercial
 Lemmings, **146–150**, *147*, *148*

Commodore Business Machines, Inc.
 and Apple II computer, 14–15
 PET computer, 15, *16*
Computer & Electronics magazine, 128
Control Data Corporation, 19
copyrights, 231, 232
corporate titles, **289**
CoStar Corporation, 195
Couch, John Dennis, 63, 67, 79, 96
CPUs. *See* microprocessors
Creative Computing magazine articles,
 128–130
credits. *See* Easter eggs
Crisp, Peter O., 118
Crow, George, 102, *106*, 164, 255, 264, 276
cursor, moving, 174

D

Daniels, Bruce, 64
Dantz Development Corporation, 196
Darooge, Bill, 194
DART (Disk Archive/Retrieval Tool) Easter
 eggs, 229
Dayna Communications, Inc., 197
dBASE Mac software, 189
Dee, Avery, 209
Delta Tao Software, 198
DeltaPoint Corporation, 197–198
Deluxe Corporation, 144
Denman, Donn, 20, 21, 276, 289
Derossi, Chris, 220, 223
Derringer code name, 228
develop magazine, 216, 224, 226
discontinuance, of Macintosh computers,
 138–141
Disk Archive/Retrieval Tool (DART) Easter
 eggs, 229
DiskDoubler software, 180
dogcow icon, **216–226**, *216. See also* icons
 origin of, 217–218
 paraphernalia, 222–223
 Tech Note #31
  distribution of, 221–222
  origin of, 218–220

trivia, 223–224
downloading files, 182
Dream, Raymond, 205–206
Drew Pictures Corporation, 199
drinks, caffeine in, **185–187**

E

Easter eggs, **227–237**
    AppleFax modem, 227–228
    Balloon Help menu, 228
    Cache Switch control panel, 228
    Caps Lock file icon, 228
    Color control panel, 229
    defined, **227**
    Disk Archive/Retrieval Tool (DART), 229
    erotic art, 232–233
    FaxMaker, 229
    "Help! Help! We're being held prisoner
       in a system software factory!"
       message, 236
    "I want my l—k and f—l" message, 234
    Installer, 229
    Labels control panel, 230
    Macintosh Classic, 230
    Macintosh IIci, 230–231
    Macintosh IIfx, 231
    Macintosh Plus, 231
    Macintosh SE, 232
    Macintosh SE/30, 232
    MacPaint 2.0 software, 232–233
    MacsBug, 233
    Map control panel, 233
    Memory control panel, 233
    Monitors control panel, 233–234
    MultiFinder, 234
    PowerBook, 234
    QuickTime, 234
    ResEdit, 234–235
    Simple Player, 235
    "Stolen from Apple Computer" message,
       231, 232
    System 6.0.7J, 235
    System 7, 228, 229, 230, 233–234,
       235–236
    System file, 236

TeachText, 236
"This file provides programmers with
    information proving that it really was
    a hardware problem" message, 233
"WHAT ARE YOU STARING AT?"
    message, 232
EasyFlow software, 152–154
Ehardt, Joseph L., 73
Eisenstat, Al, 42
Elliott, Jay, 31
e-mail addresses, author's, **237**
erotic art, 232–233
Espinosa, Chris, 41, *85*, *101*, 102, 103–104,
    106, 277
Esslinger, Hartmut, 260
Ethernet, 60–61
Excel. *See* Microsoft Excel

F

Farallon Computing, 199–200
FaxMaker Easter eggs, 229
Feldman, Dan, 188
Feldman, David N., 235
Fenton, Jay, 202
Fernandez, Bill, 4, 41, 277
Fifth Generation Systems, 207
"This file provides programmers with
    information proving that it really was
    a hardware problem" message, 233
files
    downloading, 182
    opening, 183
Finder, 106
floppy disk drives, in Lisa computer, 72
floppy disk stories, 180–182
Folon, Jean-Michel, 82–83
Fong, Norman, 200
Fontographer software, 192
fonts, 224
Fortune 500, Apple Computer enters, 46
4th Dimension software, 189
Fradin, David, 35–36
Franklin Computer Corporation, 252
Frankston, Robert, 16
frogdesign, 260

FWB, Inc., 200
Fylstra, Daniel, 16–17

G

Gagnon, Jim, 188
Gassée, Jean-Louis, 77
    on Apple III computer, 33
    on Apple logo, 9
    on IBM, 49, 124
    on Lisa computer, 76
    and Macintosh Office, 145–146, *146*
    and Sculley, 162
Gates, William Henry ("Bill"). *See also*
        Microsoft
    American Express card story, 142–144
    and Apple's Franklin Computer
        Corporation lawsuit, 252
    and MacBASIC, 19–21, 21
    and Microsoft Windows, **244–249**, 254
        development of, 246–247, 254
        licenses Macintosh technology from
            Apple, 247–249, 252
        and Macintosh software development,
            106, 244–245
    and T/Maker, 142–144
    and VisiCalc software, 17
Geschke, Dr. Charles, 189
Goldberg, Aaron, 54
Goldberg, Steve, 289
Gow, Gordon, 86
graphical user interfaces (GUIs). *See also*
        Microsoft Windows
    Lisa computer and, 66, 68, *70*
    Macintosh computer and, 88–89
    VisiOn software and, 19
    Xerox Palo Alto Research Center (PARC)
        and, 60–6

H

Haeberli, Martin P., 277, 289
Harbors, Jeff, 244
Harlan, Mark, 216–225, 225
Harvey, James, 204

Hautemont, Eric, 205–206
HavenTree Software, 152–154
Hawkins, William ("Trip"), III, 44, 59, 63,
        66, *67*, 80
Hayden, Steve, 115, 122, 124, 125, 148
"Help! Help! We're being held prisoner
        in a system software factory!"
        message, 236
Help menu Easter eggs, 228
Hertzfeld, Andy, 93, 97, 101, *106*, 278, 289
Hewlett, William, 11
Hewlett-Packard
    and Apple I computer, 11
    NewWave interface, 250, 252
Hoffman, Joanna, 105, *106*, 278
Holt, Rod, 40, 41, 278
Home Pong video game, 12
Horn, Bruce, 106, 279
Horn, Harrison S., 279
House Industries, 152, 154–155
Howard, Brian R., 279
Huffman, Drew, 199
Hughes, Tom, 83

I

"I want my l—k and f—l" message, 234
IBM, **47–58**
    Apple Computer alliance, **56–58**, *57*
    PCs
        introduction of, **47–52**
        Macintosh and, 55, 101–102
        PCjr ad, 123–124
        VisiOn software and, 19
    PowerPC chip, 56, 58
    icons
        dogcow, **216–226**, 216
        origin of, 217–218
        paraphernalia, 222–223
        Tech Note #31, 218–222
        trivia, 223–224
    in Lisa computer, 68
inCider magazine, 130–131
InfoWorld magazine, 131
initial public offering (IPO), Apple

Computer, 37–38, 41, 42, 93
Inline Software, 200–201
Inman, Admiral Bobby ("Ray"), 157
Installer Easter eggs, 229
introduction
    of IBM PC, 47–52
    of Lisa computer, 69–71
    of Macintosh computers, **72–75**,
        105–106, **136–141**
    of NeXT computer, 258–261, *258*

J

Jackson, Charlie, 208–209
Janov, Rob, 8–9
Jernigan, Ginger, 217
Jobs, Lisa, 79
Jobs, Paul R. and Clara, 2
Jobs, Steven Paul ("Steve"), *85*, **255–271**,
    280
    and *1984* commercial, 114, 116,
        117–118, 120, 123
    and Apple Computer stock, 38
    on Apple employees, 171
    and Apple I computer, 3–7, 12–14,
        37, 155
    and Apple II computer, 14–15, 260
    and Apple III computer, 30, 31–32, 66
    and Apple logo, 8–9
    on Apple's Windows lawsuit, 251
    and Breakout video game, 22–24
    and founding of Apple Computer, 1–7,
        1, 37–38, 83, 193
    and IBM PC, 48, 51, 54, 55
    and *Lemmings* commercial, 149
    and Lisa computer
        and Macintosh development,
            75–76, 77
        origin of code name, 25, **79–80**
        origin of, 59
    and project management, 66–69, 70,
        71, 93
    and Xerox Palo Alto Research Center
        (PARC), 62–65
    and Macintosh computer

and code name, 86–87, 94
and Gates, **244–246**
logo, 82–83
mouse, 97
opposition to, 84, 89
and price, 90–91
as project manager, 55, 93–97,
    100–105
and Raskin, 93–95, 100, 105, 113
and NASA, 164
and NeXT computer, **255–271**, 280
    financing, 270–271
    initial sales, 262, 269
    introduction of, 258–261, *258*
    logo, 261–262, *261*
    NeXTstation, 263–265, *263*
    NEXTSTEP operating system, 265–266,
        265, 268–269
    Perot and, 264, 265, 270–271
    startup, 255–258
    timeline, 267–268
and origin of Apple Computer's name,
    193, 238
and Perot, 264, 265, 270–271
and Sculley
    hiring Sculley, 156, 158
    Jobs' resignation, 164–167
    relationship between, 159–163, *161*
sells Apple stock, **257**
and stock options, 39–41, 42
and VisiCalc software, 16–17
and Xerox Palo Alto Research Center
    (PARC), 62–65
Johnson, Bob, 200
Johnson, Camille, 119
Johnson, Mark, 218–219, 221, 222, 223
Jolt Cola, **185–187**
Jones, Reese, 199–200

K

Kahn, Philippe, 133, 251
Kaleida Corporation, 57
Kare, Susan, 217, 224, 273
Kawasaki, Guy, 107, 108, *109*, 189, 266, 289

Kay, Alan, 50, *64*, 65, 66, 136
Kenyon, Larry, 280
King, Patti, 280
Kingman, Ray, 197–198
Kiwi SOFTWARE, 201–202
Koalkin, Barbara, 66, 103, 111
Kohl, Louise, 260
Kottke, Daniel G., 4, 39–41, *40*, 281
Kuehler, Jack, 57, *57*
Kurta Corporation, 202
Kusek, Dave, 205
Kvamme, E. Floyd, 119–120

L

Labels control panel Easter eggs, 230
laptops. *See* PowerBook computers
LaserWriter printer
    dogcow icon, **216–226**, *216*
    Macintosh Office and, 145–146, *145*
LAW (Lawyers Are Wimps) code name, 243
lawsuits. *See also* trademark battles
    Apple versus Franklin Computer
        Corporation, 252
    Apple versus Jobs, 256
    Apple versus Microsoft (Windows), 247,
        250–252
    Sculley and Spectrum Information
        Technologies, 171
Lemmings commercial, **146–150**, *147*, *148*
Lewin, Dan'l, 164, 255, 264
license agreements, **152–155**
    HavenTree Software, 152–154
    House Industries, 152, 154–155
Linzmayer, Owen W., addresses, 237
Lisa computer, **59–80**, *70*
    development of, **59–68**
    discontinued, **75–77**, *78*
    failure of, 53, 55, 71–73
    floppy disk drives, 72
    IBM PC and, 53, 55
    icons in, 68
    introduction of, **69–71**
    Jobs and
        and Macintosh development,
            75–76, 77

origin of code name, 25, **79–80**
    origin of, 59
    and project management, 66–69, 70,
        71, 93
    and Xerox Palo Alto Research Center
        (PARC), 62–65
    Lisa 2 computer, *72*, 73
    Macintosh and, 72–75
    origin of name, 25, **79–80**
    Scott and, 67–68
    timeline, **74–75**
    Xerox Palo Alto Research Center (PARC)
        and, **59–65**
Lo, Angeline, 281
Lo, Vincent, 229
logos
    Apple, 8–9, *8*, *9*
    Macintosh, **81–83**, *81*, *82*
    Newton, 240–241, *240*
    NeXT, 261–262, *261*
    Wheels for the Mind, 94, *94*
Louv, Don, 289
Lubow, Allen, 212
Luehrmann, Arthur, 21

M

MacBASIC, **19–21**
McCammon, Mary Ellen, 282
McDonald, Will, 200
Mach, Ivan, 281
Macintosh computers, **84–141**
    1984 commercial, **114–126**
        airing of, 120–123
        Big Brother's speech, 125–126, *125*
        Jobs and, 114, 116, 117–118, 120, 123
        and Macintosh price, 109
        origin of, 114–115
        Ridley Scott and, 117, 125
        Sculley and, 116, 117–119, 122
        storyboard, 115–116, *115*, *116*
        Wozniak and, 120
    Big Mac project, 164
    code names, 26, **86–87**, **241–243**
    development timeline, **104**

discontinuance of, **138–141**
Easter eggs, **230–232**
evolution of, **98–99**
Gates and, **244–249**, 252
  develops software for, 244–246
  licenses technology from Apple,
    247–249, 252
giveaway to celebrities, 110
IBM PC and, 55, 101–102
introduction of, **72–75**, 105–106,
  136–141
Jobs and
  and code name, 86–87, 94
  and Gates, **244–246**
  and mouse, 97
  opposition to, 84, 89
  and price, 90–91
  as project manager, 55, 93–97,
    100–106
  and Raskin, 93–95, 100, 105, 113
logo, **81–83**, *81*, *82*
Macintosh Classic
  Easter eggs, 230
  trademark battle, 239–240
Macintosh II trademark dispute, 239
Macintosh IIci Easter eggs, 230–231
Macintosh IIfx Easter eggs, 231
Macintosh Plus
  Easter eggs, 231
  trademark dispute, 239
Macintosh Quadra 610 DOS Compatible
  computer, 54
Macintosh SE
  Easter eggs, 232
  trademark dispute, 239
Macintosh SE/30 Easter eggs, 232
Macintosh XL computer, 75, 76–77, 80
magazine articles about, **127–135**,
  241–242
  Byte, 127–128
  Computer & Electronics, 128
  Creative Computing, 128–130
  inCider, 130–131
  InfoWorld, 131
  MacWEEK, 241–242
  Microcomputing, 131–132

*Seybold Report on Professional
  Computing*, 134–135
manufacture date of, 132
Markkula and, 84–85, 100
Microsoft Windows and, **244–252**
model introduction and exit timeline,
  136–141
monitor, 102–103
mouse, 97, 100
Power Macintosh 7100/66 code name,
  241–243
prices of, 90–91, 109, **138–141**
Raskin and, **84–95**, *85*, 97, 100
  and code names, 26, 86–87
  conception, 84–91
  and Jobs, 93–95, 100, 105, 113
  and mouse, 97, 100
  and price, 90–91
  as project manager, 91–95
  recognition of, 111
  resignation, 100
sales figures, 111
serial numbers, 132
signatures in, 100, **272–273**
software development, 106, **107–108**,
  244–245
stories, **173–184**
  After Dark software, 183
  "Any" key, 179
  bomb icon, 184
  CD-ROMs, 184
  closing windows, 179
  DiskDoubler software, 180
  downloading files, 182
  floppy disks, 180–182
  magnifying glass tool, 178
  mouse, 175, 176, 177
  mouse pads, 173–174
  moving cursor, 174
  opening files, 183
  printers, 178
  trackballs, 175
  word processors, 177, 181
  WriteNow software, 181
timelines
  development timeline, **104**

model introduction and exit timeline, **136–141**

Wozniak and, 92

McIntosh Laboratory, 86–87

Macintosh Office

Lemmings commercial, **146–150**, *147, 148*

overview of, **145–146**, *145, 146*

MacPaint software, 106, 232–233

MacroMind, 202

MacsBug Easter eggs, 233

MacUser magazine, 260

MacWEEK magazine, 241–242

MacWorks software, 75

MacWrite software, 106

magazine articles about Macintosh computers, **127–135**, 241–242

Byte, 127–128

Computer & Electronics, 128

Creative Computing, 128–130

inCider, 130–131

InfoWorld, 131

MacWEEK, 241–242

Microcomputing, 131–132

Seybold Report on Professional Computing, 134–135

magnifying glass tool, 178

Major, Anya, 117

Mandel, Alfred J., 240–241

Manock, Jerrold C., 100, *106*, 282

Manutius, Aldus, 190–191

Map control panel Easter eggs, 233

Markkula, Armas Clifford ("Mike")

and 1984 commercial, 118

and Apple III computer, 33, 34, 35

and founding of Apple Computer, 6–7, 7, 37–38

and growth of Apple Computer, 46

on IBM, 48

and Jobs' resignation, 164–166

and Macintosh computer, 84–85, 100

and Sculley, 156–157

and stock options, 41, 43

and VisiCalc software, 16

Memory control panel Easter eggs, 233

messages. See Easter eggs

Microcomputing magazine, 131–132

MicroMat Computer Systems, 203

microprocessors

6502 microprocessor, 15

6809E microprocessor, 93, 96

68000 microprocessor, 93, 96–97, 105

RISC (reduced instruction set computer) chip, 56

Microsoft BASIC, 19–21, 246

Microsoft Corporation. *See also* Gates

Apple Computer and, 56, 57

origin of name, 203

Microsoft Excel

naming of, 26

Windows development and, 247–249

Microsoft MultiPlan, 246, 249

Microsoft Windows, **244–254**

development of, 246–247

licensing lawsuits, 247, 250–252

Macintosh software development and, 244–245

Macintosh technology licensed from Sculley, 247–249, 252

timeline, 253–254

version 4 (Chicago), 252

Microsoft Windows NT, 268

Microsoft Word, 247–249

Midas code name, 137

Milledge, Vicki, 282

Modular Computer Systems Inc., 240

monitors, Macintosh, 102–103

Monitors control panel Easter eggs, 233–234

MOS Technology, 15

mouse

Macintosh, 97, 100

stories about, 173–174, 175, 176, 177

Xerox and, 61

mouse pads, 173–174

moving, cursor, 174

MultiFinder Easter eggs, 234

multimedia development, 56–58

MultiPlan software, 246

Murphy, Michael, 260

Murray, Mike, 118, 148, 149, 283

Mutter, David, 229

Mysterium Tremendum, 204

N

names, origin of, **188–215**, **224**. *See also*
    code names
  Abacus Concepts, 188
  ACIUS, 189
  Adobe Systems, 189
  Advanced Gravis, 190
  Aldus Corporation, 190–191
  Altsys Corporation, 191–192
  Ambrosia Software, 192
  Apple Computer, 193, 238
  Baudville Corporation, 194
  Broderbund Software, Inc., 194–195
  CE Software, 195
  CoStar Corporation, 195
  Dantz Development Corporation, 196
  Dayna Communications, Inc., 197
  Delta Tao Software, 198
  DeltaPoint Corporation, 197–198
  Drew Pictures Corporation, 199
  Farallon Computing, 199–200
  of fonts, **224**
  FWB, Inc., 200
  Inline Software, 200–201
  Kiwi SOFTWARE, 201–202
  Kurta Corporation, 202
  MacroMind, 202
  MicroMat Computer Systems, 203
  Microsoft Corporation, 203
  Mysterium Tremendum, 204
  Opcode Systems Inc., 205
  Passport Designs, 205
  Radius Corporation, 206
  RasterOps Corporation, 207
  Ray Dream, Inc., 205–206
  Sentient Software, 207–208
  Shiva Corporation, 208
  Silicon Beach Software, 208–209
  Silicon Valley Bus Company, 209
  Sir-Tech Software, 210
  Software Toolworks, 210
  STF Technologies, 211
  Strata Corporation, 211–212
  SYNEX Corporation, 212
  Teknosys Corporation, 213

  Thunderware, 214
  Timeworks International, 214
  T/Maker, 215
Nathan, John, 270
National Aeronautics and Space
    Administration (NASA), 164
Newmark, Andrew, 195
Newsweek advertising insert, 124
Newton logo, 240–241, *240*
NewWave interface, 250, 252
NeXT computer, 113, **255–271**. *See also*
    Jobs
  financing, 270–271
  initial sales, 262, 269
  introduction of, 258–261, *258*
  logo, 261–262, *261*
  NeXTstation, 263–265, *263*
  NEXTSTEP operating system, 265–266,
    265, 268–269
  Perot and, 264, 265, 270–271
  Raskin and, 113
  startup, 255–258
  timeline, 267–268
Nicholson, Ronald H., Jr., 283
Norman, David, 262
nudes, 232–23

O

Opcode Systems Inc., 205
opening files, 183
Oppenheim, Dave, 205
origin of names. *See* names
Oyama, Terry A., 283

P

P.C. Letter, 260
Packard, David, 11
Page, Richard, 63, 164, 167, 255, 264
Page Setup dialog box. *See* dogcow icon
PageMaker software, 190–191
Pake, George, 65
Palo Alto Research Center (PARC), Xerox,
    59–66, *60*

Pang, Benjamin, 284
Passport Designs, 205
PCs. *See also* IBM
    introduction of, **47–52**
    Macintosh and, 55, 101–102
    PCjr ad, 123–124
    VisiOn software and, 19
PDM (Piltdown Man) code name, 241, 243
Peck, Darryl, 200–201
Peddle, Chuck, 15
Pepsi code name, 80
Pepsi-Cola, 157, 158, 186
Performa computers, 136
Perot, H. Ross, 264, 265, 270–271
Personal Software, Inc., 16, 19
PET computer, 15, *16*
Petaccia, Tom, 174
Petrie, Tom, 214
pig mode, ResEdit, 234–235
Piltdown Man (PDM) code name, 241, 243
Pink operating system, 56–58, 268
Pizzuti, Louella, 218
Pong video game, 12, 22
Power Macintosh 7100/66 code name,
    241–243
PowerBook computers
    code names for, 228
    Easter eggs, **234**
    model 540/540c, 137
PowerPC computers, 56, 58
press. *See* magazine articles
prices
    of Apple Computer stock, 45
    of Apple I computer, 155
    of Macintosh computers, 90–91, 109,
        138–141
    of Performa computers, 136
    suggested retail prices (SRPs) versus
        ApplePrices, 136
printers, stories about, 178
processors. *See* microprocessors
programmers. *See* Easter eggs

Q

QuickDraw software, 62
QuickTime Easter eggs, 234

R

Radius Corporation, 206
Rainey, Mary Terese, 121
Rand, Paul, 261–262
Rapp, C.J., 186
Raskin, Jef, **84–95**, 97, 100, 284
    and Canon Cat, 112–113, *112*
    and Lisa computer, 62–63, 64
    and Macintosh computer, **84–95**, *85*,
        97, 100
    code name, 26, **86–87**
    conception, 84–91
    and Jobs, 93–95, 100, 105, 113
    and mouse, 97, 100
    price, 90–91
    as project manager, 91–95
    recognition of, 111
    resignation, 100
    profile, **284**
RasterOps Corporation, 207
Ray Dream, Inc., 205–206
reduced instruction set computer (RISC)
    chip, 56
ResEdit Easter eggs, 234–235
Ricard, Yann, 201–202
Riddle, Ed, 284
RISC (reduced instruction set computer)
    chip, 56
Rizzo, Paul, 260
Robertson, Brian, 285
Roche, Gerry, 159
Rock, Arthur, 118
Roizen, J.A. Heidi, 142–144, 215
Roots, David H., 285
Rosen, Ben, 87
Rossman, Alain, 206
Rothmuller, Ken, 59, 63, 66, 71, 79–80
Russell, Grant, 190

S

Sadlier, Bill, 197
Sagan, Carl, 241–243
sales
  of Macintosh computers, 111
  of NeXT computer, 262, 269
Sand code name, 244
Sander, Wendell, 28
Sara code name, 28
Schiller, Vic, 214
Schlein, Philip S., 118
Schwinn, Dan, 208
Scott, Michael M., *85*
  on Apple logo, 9
  and Apple reorganizations, 67–68, 75,
    93, 156
  and Lisa computer, 63, 67–68, 93
  and stock options, 41
Scott, Ridley, 117, 125, 146
Scott, Tony, 146, 147
Scott-Jackson, Dennis, 190
Sculley, John, **156–172**, *157*
  and *1984* commercial, 116, 117–119,
    122
  and Apple advertising, 122, 124
  business card, **289**
  and dogcow icon, 218
  and IBM alliance, 56–58, *57*
  on IBM PC, 52, 53
  and Jobs
    hiring Sculley, 156, 158
    relationship between, 159–163, *161*
    resignation of, 164–167
  after Jobs' resignation, **167–168**
  joins Apple Computer, 75, **156–158**,
    159, 160
  and *Lemmings* commercial, 148–149
  licenses Macintosh technology to
    Microsoft, **247–249**, 252
  and Macintosh computer, 109, 110
  replaced as CEO, **168**
  and Spectrum Information
    Technologies, **169–171**
  timeline, **172**
secret messages. *See* Easter eggs

Sentient Software, 207–208
Seybold, Andrew, 168
Seybold Report on Professional Computing,
    134–135
Sharp, Patricia, 285
Shayer, David, 207–208
Shiva Corporation, 208
signatures, in Macintosh computers, 100,
    272–273
Silicon Beach Software, 208–209
Silicon Valley Bus Company, 209
Silver Surfer code name, 189
Simple Player Easter eggs, 235
Singleton, Dr. Henry E., 118
Sirotek, Fred, 210
Sir-Tech Software, 210
Skeie, Dick, 195
Slaughter, Frank, 208
Smalltalk language, 61, 64
Smith, Burrell Carver
  business card, 289
  and Macintosh computer, 91–92, 96,
    100, *106*
  profile, 286
  and Radius Corporation, 206
Smoot, Steve, 213
software development, for Macintosh, 106,
    107–108, 244–245
Software Toolworks, 210
Sorenson, Keith, 207
Spectrum Information Technologies,
    169–171
Spindler, Michael ("Diesel"), 168, *168*
spreadsheet software
  Microsoft Excel, 26, 247–249
  VisiCalc, **16–19**, *18*, 47
Sproull, Newman, 207
Spruce Goose code name, 137
SRPs (suggested retail prices), 136
StatView software, 188
Stearns, Bryan, 286
Stearns, Robert W., 58
STF Technologies, 211
stock (Apple)
initial public offering (IPO), 37–38, 41,
    42, 93

Jobs sells, **257**
price history, **45**
stock options, **37–43**
stock symbols, 44
"Stolen from Apple Computer" message,
    231, 232
stories, **173–184**
    After Dark software, 183
    "Any" key, 179
    bomb icon, 184
    CD-ROMs, 184
    closing windows, 179
    DiskDoubler software, 180
    downloading, 182
    floppy disks, 180–182
    magnifying glass tool, 178
    mouse, 175, 176, 177
    mouse pads, 173–174
    moving cursor, 174
    opening files, 183
    printers, 178
    trackballs, 175
    word processors, 177, 181
    WriteNow software, 181
Strata Corporation, 211–212
Subramaniam, Sriram, 220
suggested retail prices (SRPs), 136
Super Bowl commercials
    1984, **114–126**
    Lemmings, **146–150**, *147, 148*
SYNEX Corporation, 212
System 6.0.7J Easter eggs, 235
System 7
    Blue Meanies quality-control team,
        234, 236
    Easter eggs, 228, 229, 230, 233–234,
        235–236
System file Easter eggs, 236

T

Takahashi, Lynn, 286
Taligent Corporation, 57, 268
TeachText Easter eggs, 236
Tech Note #31, 216, 218–222
Teknosys Corporation, 213

Terrell, Paul, 3–4
Tesler, Lawrence G., 64, 66
"This file provides programmers with
    information proving that it really was
    a hardware problem" message, 233
Thomas, Brent, 115
Thunderware, 214
TIM code name, 228
timelines
    Lisa computer, 74–75
    Macintosh
      development timeline, 104
      model introduction and exit timeline,
        136–141
    Microsoft Windows, 253–254
    NeXT computer, 267–268
    John Sculley, **172**
Timeworks International, 214
titles, business, **289**
T/Maker Corporation
    Gates and, 142–144
    origin of name, 215
Tognazzi, Bruce, 78
trackballs, 175
Trackpad, 137
trademark battles, **238–243**. *See also*
    lawsuits
    Apple Computer versus Apple Corps,
      238–239
    Carl Sagan code name, 241–243
    Macintosh Classic, 239–240
    Newton logo, 240–241, *240*
Tramiel, Jack, 15
Tribble, Guy L., III ("Bud"), 82, 164, 255,
    264, 287
Troxell, Doug, 211
Trujillo, Toni, 223
Tung, Kenny S. C., 235
Twiggy floppy drives, 72

V

Valentine, Don, 6
VisiCalc software, **16–19**, *18*, 47
VisiCorp, Inc., 19

VisiOn software, 19
Von Ehr, Jim, 191–192

W

Warner Communications, 13
Warnock, Dr. John, 189
Wayne, Ron
  and Apple logo, 8
  and founding of Apple Computer, 1–7
Welch, Andrew, 192
"WHAT ARE YOU STARING AT?"
  message, 232
Wheels for the Mind promotion, 94, *94*
Whitney, Dr. Thomas M., 63–64
Wigginton, Randy, 19, 30, 41, 106, 287
Wilcox, Jim, 211
Wilkin, Linda, 287
Williams, Joe, 198
Windows. *See* Microsoft Windows
windows, closing, 179
word processors
  Canon Cat, 112–113, *112*
  Microsoft Word, 247–249
  stories about, 177, 181
  WriteNow, 142–144, 181
WordStar International, 144
Wozniak, Jerry, 14, 41
Wozniak, Stephen Gary ("Steve"), *85*
  and *1984* commercial, 120
  and Apple Computer stock, 38
  and Apple I computer, 11–14, 37, 155
  and Apple II computer, 14–15
  and Apple III computer, 30, 34
  and Breakout video game, 22–24
  and founding of Apple Computer, 1–7,
    37–38, 83

  on Jobs, 91, 152
  on Lisa code name, 79
  and Macintosh computer, 92
  on NeXT computer, 269
  and origin of Apple Computer's name,
    193, 238
  profile, **288**
  and stock options, 41, 42–43
  WozPlan stock options, 42–43
WriteNow software
  Gates and, 142–144
  story about, 181
Wyman, Pamela G., 288

X

Xerox Corporation, **59–66**
  Alto computer, 60–65, *61*
  and Ethernet, 60–61
  mouse and, 61
  Palo Alto Research Center (PARC),
    59–66, *60*
  Smalltalk language, 61, 64

Y

Yu, Dean, 229

Z

zebras, 232–233
Zimmerman, Scott ("Zz"), 217, 220, 222, 223
Zsidek, Laslo, 288
Zulch, Larry and Richard, 196

FREE SAMPLE DISK

If you like *The Mac Bathroom Reader*, check out these other fun books by the same author, each containing an 800K disk with cool programs:

Totally Rad Mac Programs

Customizes desktop patterns, Apple menu icons, shut down procedures, startup screens, animations, and messages. Also links sound effects to actions, sings "99 Bottles of Beer," replaces menu bar text with neat icons, blinks lights on extended keyboards, tears windows, makes Kilroy pop up, saves screen, bounce windows on desktop, says "Makin' Copies," and more.

21 programs, 138 pages

Bitchin' Mac Programs

Customizes cursors, icons, menu bar patterns, system fonts, background colors, shut down procedures, and startup messages. Also plays songs in the background, announces the time, pronounces text in dialog boxes, spawns fish on desktop, bounces ball in menu bar, spins folders into place, strings lights from menu bar, causes ditigal snowstorms on the desktop, and much more.

17 programs, 135 pages

For your *free* disk containing sample programs from each book along with complete instructions, send a self-addressed, stamped, envelope to:

Owen Ink Sample Disk
2227 15th Avenue
San Francisco, CA 94116-1824

(Limit one per household)

Cyan, Inc.
P.O. Box 28096
Spokane, WA 99228

509–468–0807
Fax: 509-467-2209
AppleLink: CYAN

April 25, 1994

Mr. Owen Linzmayer
2227 15th Avenue

San Francisco, CA 94116

Dear Mr. Linzmayer,

Blah, blah blah blah blah Cyan blah Blah blah *Myst* blah Blah. BLAH! Blah blah blah blah blah blah blah blah, blah blah blah blah. Blah blah blah blah blah blah: blah blah. Blah blah Cyan blah blah blah blah blahblah blah blah blah blah Myst blah blah. Blahblah *The Manhole Masterpiece Edition* blah blah blah *Cosmic Osmo and the Worlds Beyond the Mackerel*.

The Manhole Masterpiece Edition blah blah blah blah blah blahblah blah blah blah blahblah blah. Blahblah blah blah blah. Blah blah blah blahblah; blah blah blah blah blah. Blah blah blah *The Manhole Masterpiece Edition*, blah blah blah blah blah blah blahblah blahblah.

Cosmic Osmo and the Worlds Beyond the Mackerel blah blah blah blah blah blah blah blah blahblah blah blah, blah blah. Blah blah! Blah blah blah & blah blah blah blah blah, blah blah blah blah blah blah blah blah. Blah, *Cosmic Osmo and the Worlds Beyond the Mackerel* blah blah blah blah blah blah blah blah blah blah blah blah blahblah. Blah blah - blah blah. Blah blah blah blah blah blah blah blah blah blah blahblah. Blah blah.

Blah blah Cyan blah blah blah blah blah blah blahblah blah - blah blah. Blah blah blah blah blah blah blah blah blah blah blahblah.

Regards,

Rand Miller & Robyn Miller
Founders

P.S. Blah blah blah blah blah Blah blah: blah blah blah!